CONCEAL REVEAL

CONCEAL REVEAL

THE SPACE BETWEEN ENTREPRENEURS AND THE DEFENSE INDUSTRY

JULIE WILLIS

NEW DEGREE PRESS

CONCEAL REVEAL

The Space Between Entrepreneurs And The Defense Industry

ISBN   978-1-63676-586-0 *Paperback*

978-1-63676-217-3 *Kindle Ebook*

978-1-63676-212-8 *Ebook*

Dedication

To everyone who supported me during this journey–thank you. Your name may not be in the book, but your presence in my life made it happen. From family and friends, old colleagues and new connections... my heart is full.

CONTENTS

———

Dear Warfighter,

Thank you for making it possible for me to sleep peacefully last night.

I hope you to know that feeling, too.

Love,

Julie

INTRODUCTION

———

I've spent my career playing the role of the nice girl who doesn't rock the boat. In fact, I'm pretty good at steadying metaphorical boats. Is it any surprise why I'm afraid to rock the boat now? I don't know how to extend my arm, point at the issue, and shout, "We have a big problem!"

That said, I'm going to do the best I can, and along the way, I'll show you the journey I've taken in 2020 from being a government contractor to becoming an entrepreneur in the defense industry. I'll also unzip my chest and show you why my heart beats for this mission.

My publisher has told me three times I need to come up with the goal of writing this book—not the "why" but the "what" I want out of it. I know what's holding me back from saying it out loud is imposter syndrome, and I'd like to get that out of the way now.

Who the hell am I to dare to point out a flaw in the system that keeps our country safe?

(sips tea)

I'm a nobody. I'm an outsider. I've never worn a uniform. I'm pretty sure I couldn't pass a physical fitness test if I had to. I am just Julie.

So, what value does Julie bring? Why should anyone care what she thinks? She's never even written an entire document in all capitals, a rite of passage in the defense industry.

You know who she thinks should write this book? The people in charge. Or maybe they should focus on taking their own advice and implementing the recommendations their peers have come up with. They are the players who occupy the layers (as discussed in Chapter 10) of bureaucracy. Since they either can't or won't, she will.

Ahem, I will.

Know what I want? I want this to be read by someone who can add it to a growing pile of evidence proving more needs to be done to fight corruption in government spending. Whether that is a staffer on the hill or an internal change agent, I really don't care. If you are that someone, please let me know. I want this book to be digestible for folks who would never pick up doctrine or policy. (Because why would you?) I want it to keep the spark alive in the disillusioned.

I want it to inspire you. To do what? That's up to you.

So, what do I know about military modernization? What leg do I have to stand on? I'll tell you a little secret that'll make a few of you uncomfortable: I've been paying attention the entire time. I may not have been the influential one in the room or one of the players at the table, but I was there. This is not a book about not having a voice or the one time I dared to ask a four-star general a question in a briefing (which is a great story for another book).

Instead, this is the book that forces Uncle Sam to see an accepted practice through a new perspective. Uncle Sam needs to know I see the picture differently now that I've been on both sides. Like so many in the defense industry, I continue to show up in spite of what I see.

I remember crying crocodile tears in front of the Command Sergeant Major (CSM) after he delivered a speech I wrote for an event. It is not customary for contractors to attend events, even those their work contributes to. The poor man asked me why I bought a ticket. That's it. He asked it in the way only a seasoned CSM of a four-star command can do. He looked me in the eye, from what felt like a foot above me, asking half a dozen times until I told him the truth. I tried to give him little answers, but he was not satisfied. "I'm here because this matters," I said. "Why," he responded, and not with a question mark, but with a period. Why.

I had a coach in graduate school who tried to help me find my "why." She would not accept my "why" was simply "because they're dying." I have a soft spot for people caught in situations that don't need to be fatal like refugees, reporters, warfighters, and civilians. We spent session after session on this. Eventually, we landed on something else, but I don't remember it, probably because they're dying. Seriously, they're dying. If that's not a call to action, I don't know what is.

So, the CSM got the animated answer complete with flailing arms and big crocodile tears. There was swearing, sniffling, and big exhales. And there was truth. I was there because they're dying. The people who do the thing that keeps us from dying? They're dying, and the least we can do is do the best we can do.

And then, I got mad because ain't nobody got time for the bullshit. There was resistance to me and my why, if you can believe it. Inside the system. The people who asked, "Why Julie? Why is Julie doing this? Who said she could? Who authorized this?" need to understand that I'm not property. I do not need permission to be here or to tell this story.

I came to the United States Army Futures Command (AFC) thinking everyone was on the same page: we are all here for the mission! I learned over and over this was not the case. I'm naive and idealistic. I thought we were here because the next generation of warfighters needed us, but I discovered there were people who needed AFC to bolster their own careers more than the next generation. I was there for a paycheck, too, no doubt about it! But I felt a responsibility with that paycheck.

The more people blocked me, or tried to block me, the more frustrated I became. I saw myself cycle between apathy and awesomeness. Very high highs and very low lows. I was heading straight for apathy and not happy about it. "Why are people getting in my way?" I asked. The CSM asked me the same question back: "Julie, why are people getting in your way?"

Oh, shit. This launched the "If you're not here to get the warfighter what they need, get the fuck out of the way of the people who are" speech. He listened and offered nothing other than an ear. Military modernization needs more of those moments. It needs more people like this CSM. It needs more people willing to stand up and say this is not good enough; this day was not good enough. What we have done so far is great, but it's not good enough.

That's my superpower, and I can say this. Think about it from their perspective. If they're a player in a layer which will cut them a check for the rest of their life who's made it twenty-plus years, they probably can't say it is not good enough. There are consequences for them. I get that, but I don't respect it. I've refused to go down that path because I won't trade my superpower for a retirement check. I might work until I retire and never know the pleasure of asking my assistant if the registration for my yacht has come in yet. I'll just have to live with that.

In exchange for the security of a government pension, I get to have a different perspective, opinion, and voice. Because I'm a nobody—an outsider who never served—I get to do this. What's the best thing that could happen? The warfighters don't die. I realize warfighters die. Death is currency in their economy. But maybe one of them doesn't. Maybe more don't. That's what I want from this book. Ready?

PART 1

EAT, PRAY, LOVE... WAR

CHAPTER 1

GRENADE

———

The cause of war is preparation for war.

—W.E.B. DUBOIS

Today is April 24, 2020. It's a Saturday. I've had a lot of coffee. The day started innocently enough. I woke up with the goal of getting to the trail before the Austinites overran the place. There is something about Austin, Texas, that refuses to allow social distancing. Maybe it's the "we're counterculture" vibe that makes Austin awesome. The slogan is "Keep Austin Weird." It's posted all over town as well as on souvenir t-shirts across the country, but Austin is only weird relative to the rest of Texas. I have no idea WHY people run by me with six inches instead of six feet between us like they're passing on a track and can't afford the extra half step they'll have to take to make up that lost ground.

I'm up. I put on my morning uniform: favorite yoga pants, a sports bra (I know I'm just walking, but I don't want to risk sweating in a real bra), and a long-sleeve black shirt (I have an unnatural fear of weird tan lines) and add my trail shoes. They're just hiking shoes I affectionately refer to as my trail shoes so I can keep my pink Nikes as my indoor workout shoes. I live alone and have no pets, so yeah, I have a white rug (as well as a white couch, white sheets, and white towels). Momentum and the knowledge that as soon as I pop outside, I'll be at Merit carries me. Merit is the only coffee shop on the way to the trail. The special thing about Merit, other than the fact it's open, is they have Splenda. I love Trader Joe's stevia drops, and I put them in everything, but stevia in green packets is bitter. It's supposed to be a sweetener, right? Who did this? My best guess is some guy named Bob at the product meeting said, "If we put it in the green packets, people will think it's more natural and will forgive how awful it is." Thanks, Bob. Splenda, on the other hand, is happiness. I've bought giant bags of it and poured them into bowls, added water, stirred, and eaten the sticky goo. I fucking love Splenda, but I don't want cancer.

First-world problems are so hard sometimes.

As soon as I'm out of my building I get a voice memo from a friend. When two people who love coffee and being outside ping each other in the morning, you know what comes next. I walked into Merit and ordered two red eyes: one double, and one single with three Splenda packets. I make a note to remind myself of how good this tastes when I am inevitably diagnosed.

Waiting outside feels awkward. I somehow feel naughty for simply waiting for a friend to appear from around the corner. So, I sit here and watch dog people try to figure out if I'm allowed to be out there waiting. Waiting in public is now taboo.

My friend arrives and we clink cups. Somewhere, many blocks later and past abandoned Austin hot spots, the coffee kicks in, and I'm ranting and raving on behalf of my clients.

"No, no, no, no. You know what the problem with modernization is? It's the fucking capture management racket behind the scenes holding all the cards," I swore a little too loudly, but it's not like anyone is around to hear me. Not familiar with capture? If you search on LinkedIn for "Capture Manager," you'll find them mostly in Washington, D.C. It's a job title for the space between companies with a product or service and the government. It's not business development and it's not contracts, but it's new business with relationships, kind of. They typically get a percentage of the contract when it's awarded, like the business development folks. So, what's the difference? Good question.

"I've been waiting for you to say that," is what I get in return. It's an "I told you so" without having told me anything. It's horribly arrogant and annoying.

"What the fuck?" I let the "I told you so" go because I'm more annoyed with the system right now. "Why is no one talking about this?"

My rant continues until I say what really bothers me. It's not the bloated grant-writing companies taking a rake off the top of research and development (R&D) that gets under my skin. They exist like a nasty bug bite you can't stop scratching. It makes me batty, but they are doing a service. My feelings on this are complicated, but so is translating engineer-speak into a document meeting government criteria. Not my battle today.

"You know what it really is? It's not the grant writing. I'm cool with that. Federal research dollars are available to anyone, if they have a magic signature. Where? On the fucking Memorandums of Understanding (MOUs). Understanding what? Oh, or call it a Letter of Support. From whom? Support of what? How have we incentivized a competitive application process that allows for supporting documents, but you have to know someone to get them? That's not cool. How are companies supposed to come up with a potential customer for their research or prototype when those folks are behind lock and key on some base in the middle of nowhere surrounded by fences and under constant surveillance?"

"Exactly," he says.

Exactly what? I'm not totally sure. I just know it feels wrong.

We've reached the end of the road. The conversation literally dead ends at the eerily silent convention center. We haven't seen another person for blocks. We look at each other and turn around, agreeing to get more coffee at Austin Java on the way back. My rant intensifies, if possible. I'm swearing like a mad woman on an abandoned apocalyptic city street about government bureaucracy. I might want to reevaluate how I spend my free time.

"What are your potential clients telling you?"

"Oh, you're going to regret asking that," I laugh. "They know the application process favors packing the small business innovation research, or SBIR, application with MOUs because they add credibility and merit. It makes sense, right?"

"How?" He asks. Not because he doesn't know, but because he wants me to say it.

"It validates the demand from inside the military." I take a deep breath thinking it through. "Okay so, let's say someone is developing a robot army... um... like *Terminator* meets the Terracotta Warriors. Before Uncle Sam cuts a check for prototype development, it would sure be nice to know if the Army wanted to buy robot soldiers, right? That's where the letters of support and MOUs come in. They would say, 'If the technology to make, manufacture, and sustain robot soldiers existed, then the Army would be interested in procuring a motherfucking robot army,' or something."

"What's the problem?" Ugh. Again, he forces me to go through the motions.

"The problem is that the system is rigged!" I'm getting frustrated having to explain this because it seems so obvious to me now. "It's nearly impossible to find the people who can sign those letters. I'm constantly asked: 'How do we meet those people?' I don't know!"

"That's not true. You do know."

I inhale.

"Fine." I exhale. "I do know. It's through the network. However, the little guy with the game-changing tech doesn't have the time to cultivate the network, so the only choice in a competitive bid process to deliver a winning proposal is to buy that MOU."

"How much does that cost?" he asks.

"So, this is where my earlier rant about the capture management companies comes in. They'll sell you access to their network inside the fence and all the way to the right person for 50 percent of the value of a Phase 1 SBIR. Oh! And read the fine print because sometimes they get a cut of everything after that. We have a system that not only allows for 'pay to play' but incentivizes it."

"How is that ethical?"

"Seriously? It's not. If they were paying government officials, it would be easy to see these as bribes. Because they're paying those officials' friends, now retired or out of the system, it's the same ethical problem with a new name. Have you heard of payola?"

"The music promotion scandal in the 1960s? Julie, you're losing me here."

I run out of steam in front of the JW Marriott. Normally we'd never be able to just walk up like this. Cars are usually trying to enter or exit the valet semi-circle. My mouth catches up to my thoughts, and I'm reminded of how many events I've been to there. How many times have I taken for granted meeting up at the lobby bar? The restaurant outside? The private pool for spa guests? Enough times to pause and let the loss of pre-COVID-19 life sink in. "Normally" doesn't apply anymore.

"Yep, that scandal. Song promoters paid radio stations and DJs to play their songs, making it look like they had popular support. Same thing here. You can buy 'popular support' for your SBIR by paying promoters to get the signatures from their buddies."

"American innovation and research are caught in the old boys club," he says and sums it up.

We reminisce about the deals we've seen happen—on golf trips, at steakhouses, and in bars. We don't get stuck talking about the sex parties like we usually do. We've talked those to death so many times neither of us cares anymore to go down that rabbit hole. We share a dismissive laugh and jaywalk across the six-lane street. Nobody is coming.

"So, I'm writing this book about modernization and my experience, right?"

"Right."

"You know I can't just NOT talk about this," I say.

"Think about that. A lot of money is tied up behind those networks. They'll discredit you. It will close this door. What about your clients?"

I sigh. I know this already. Reputation is currency in this ecosystem. One nasty comment, true or not, is all it takes to bankrupt someone. My thoughts turn to the one I heard about a former defense director just three days ago. The word 'former' is doing a lot of work in that sentence.

"Fuck. I don't know."

We order coffee at the to-go counter behind our home-sewn masks. The energy is electric. We're talking about throwing a grenade into my new business. I might have to find a different industry. Two other customers are waiting in the uncomfortable space big enough for all of us to be six feet away from each other. We don't even talk while there. The topic too sensitive, too real. This is whistleblower shit, except I don't have any evidence. Is it just wrong or wrong-wrong? I don't know. I'm not the *New York Times*. I'm not going to concoct some elaborate ruse to trap some poor schmuck in a mid-food chain career into taking the fall. I'm also not saying I wouldn't do so if I thought I could. I was a contractor in the Department of Defense's Inspector General's (IG) Office of Special Programs before my latest contract position at Army Futures Command. There is no way the IG would ignore this if they knew what was going on.

The cloak of protective idealism keeping my head from exploding starts to fail. Who am I kidding? They know what's going on.

* * *

I just got home from my coffee rant in Downtown Austin.

I guess I'm the one with the least to lose here. The only perk of being the little guy is that this likely won't make more than a ripple.

I just can't ignore the icky feeling that I might be using my talents for evil. Why blow up my new business if I'm not sure I'm the good guy? Last year, I went on a little day trip to a rural old-timey town in Texas with a colleague. I bought a few random trinkets, mostly at the antique store, and one of them was a postcard. On the front it says, "The cause of war is preparation for war." Thanks, W. E. B. DuBois. It pairs nicely with Voltaire's, "No snowflake in an avalanche ever feels responsible." Awkward.

It's reasonable to think I, Julie Willis, take responsibility for my participation in the future destruction caused by the weaponization of whatever I'm involved in. It's complicated because ultimately, I want to stop the dying, not make it more efficient. I prefer to not spend time in that rabbit hole. It's dark down there.

When I do get sidetracked and realize I'm halfway down the rabbit hole, and that does happen, I find it comforting if I flip the question. What if military technology can be de-weaponized and used for good?

The postcard lives on the shoe cabinet next to the front door. It sits between a tube of Christian Dior's iconic red lipstick and a silver flamingo statue. I tell you this for two reasons. Number one, so you know even though I don't spend time in that rabbit hole, I don't ignore it. I preach I'm in it for the warfighter, and that's true. It's also true that I think they are a last resort, and it makes me uncomfortable that we don't discuss that more often. Number two, because silver flamingo statues make great pets.

Now that I'm home, alone, over-caffeinated, and agitated, I run through the conversation I just had a few times. What else would I use my good brain for on a Saturday afternoon? I see the stupid postcard as I drop my keys into the pink enameled dish I bought in October at the JW Marriott gift shop in Palm Springs. It reads "THE FUTURE IS FEMALE."

My home is a collection of things that make me think, and together with the postcard, this dish does the job.

I can't remember when I first became aware of the icky feeling that the SBIR process is rigged. I'm trying to think how far back the signs were and what they looked like at the time. Did I just dismiss them? I know I must have seen them go by—a comment here and a comment there, clients complaining about "the system" and turning to me as if I was the keeper of the secret map through the labyrinth. Now I see so many of the pieces together, I can't unsee the full picture. Thankfully, there is something about not having access to all the pieces that keeps me safe.

Safe, yes. But quiet? No, thank you.

I make myself a double water to dilute the coffee and set up the laptop outside on the balcony. What am I doing in this industry? All I want is to get the warfighters whatever they need to do their jobs and come home. I don't want to fight "the system." The bureaucracy nearly killed my resolve last year, and I had to start completely fresh with my new company to feel like I could contribute in a meaningful way.

Ugh. Why is this so hard? I'm just a girl who loves adventure. Adventure wrote most of this book, along with my insatiable curiosity and love of hotel breakfasts. Without adventure, though, I would have missed seeing the picture take shape. It was as if every conversation I had gave me a new piece. I'm scared to say what I see, but it's corruption. Right?

I described it today, and my fear was validated. If a stack of MOUs make my R&D proposal stronger and I can just buy them, then we need to stop collecting MOUs at Phase 1. Right?

* * *

I turn my attention to my laptop and open Quip, the app used by my book writing program. I start writing a chat message to the man behind the scenes. "Hi Eric" sounds too formal and not desperate enough. Yesterday he sent me a note saying he had some time this weekend to read my intro. Oops. I haven't responded, and I've written it twice, only to abandon each version.

Julie: It would be great if we could chat. Can I use a calendar link to set it up?

Eric: I won't have time right now for calls (time is so tight with kids and work) - but happy to chat here. What's up?

Julie: I can do that. First update for you is I'm not writing the book you and I talked about.

I pause to consider how abrupt this will come across. Adding a smiley face improves it dramatically, and I continue.

Julie: It isn't the book. Instead, I am writing more of a memoir of the entrepreneur experience in the military modernization space. I hit a huge block when I tried to project the future of warfare and realized that was probably because that's not what I do.

Oh boy.

Julie: Anyway...

Eric: Cool. That's great - write the book you feel called and compelled to write. Honestly that's the only way authors finish.

Eric: I will let Lyn know so she can invite you to the creative author sessions which should be helpful with building and structuring that style of book.

Julie: I had an interesting conversation today that validated some of my thinking about the modernization process and small businesses. The only issue is that it could expose potential criminal activity.

I take a deep breath. Too much? Accurate? I think so. If access to the signatory of the MOU is kept out of reach and commoditized, how is that not illegal? It's at least unethical, but I'm no lawyer.

Julie: Thanks for the support. I want the book to add context and story to policy.

I inhale.

Julie: I'm unwilling to NOT shine a light on this issue, but I'm also not sure I want to go down that path. Mainly because I don't have evidence and I'm not the NY Times. :)

I exhale.
The smiley face is really working hard today.

Julie: It's an interesting development. I want to include and allude to it. I'm just not sure how to do that and keep from being discredited.

Oof. The risk sinks in.

Julie: So. I'll write about it and see where it goes. We can talk about it in a few days. Does that work?

Eric: Best thing is to write up your intro/authors note and share. That's the document that helps you make the case. Share it and happy to take a read. But it's the piece that really helps you make the case this book and story is compelling.

Julie: Gotcha

Julie: 100$

Typos are real, my friends.

Julie: 100% Thank you

Eric: Have you watched "Molly's Game?" It's a style called Creative Nonfiction (it's a specific type of memoir). Might be helpful for you as you structure.

Julie: The woman who ran the poker games?

Eric: Focuses on a key period and tells it in more of a "fiction like" style.

Eric: Yes.

Julie: I like that. I did watch it

Eric: So, the book could tell the story of a particular one year (or whatever period) and use flash backs and flash forwards to complement

Eric: Worth watching it or "Eat Pray Love" and documenting how they use "scenes" to organize the story.

Julie: Best stay at home binge advice ever! :)

Cheers to the emojis today.
I did not want to do anything work-related anyway. So, I cuddled up with my iPad on the bed and started to watch *Eat, Pray, Love* for the third time. I started watching it just a few months ago when Netflix had it, but since it was too close to a breakup, I didn't want to finish it. I had, however, written on my living room window in dry erase last week:

Eat

Pray

Love

Creepy.

CHAPTER 2

IT'S ABOUT THE MONEY, HONEY

———

Money is the opposite of the weather. Nobody talks about it, but everybody does something about it.

—REBECCA JOHNSON

May 1, 2020

I wake up with a song in my head every day. Today's subconscious soundtrack was brought to me by Blackbear with his popular "hot girl bummer" track. For the sake of not getting sued for copyright infringement by putting in the lyrics, I'll have to just ask you to listen to it. It's catchy.

This might be a good day to cross some items off my "shit list."

I'm up and out of bed with the intent to get outside before the Austinites hit the trail.

"Hey Siri, please have Spotify play 'hot girl bummer,'" I ask while brushing my teeth. The most important decision of my day is coming up, and I think an angry anthem is what I need to make the right call.

Do I make coffee or buy coffee?

If I buy it, I can toss the cup in a recycle bin on the trail. If I brew my own, I have to carry the travel mug.

Privilege is a bitch. I make coffee because it's not really about carrying the stupid mug. I just don't want to spend the money. I checked my email and according to my soon-to-be former bank, the Payment Protection Program (PPP) funds should be in my account within the next three business days. I'll believe it when I see it. Actually, I'll believe it when I file the paperwork later to have it forgiven.

Wait... no. I'll believe it in seven years when the government no longer cares to send me a letter requesting it back. Maybe I should push that out until the next year, just to be sure. I will sigh with relief on New Year's Day 2028.

Shit... no. What if they mail it in 2027, and it doesn't get to me until mid-January? That's totally possible and not unlikely, given the state of things. Okay. Setting a reminder on my phone to sigh on January 15, 2028. It's gonna be great.

I'm not ungrateful, I'm angry. This has been so poorly executed that I don't trust it. My ask is minuscule. It wouldn't qualify as a rounding error for other companies. That's what we'll call it—my rounding error. I interrupt Spotify to request "Started" so Iggy Azalea and I can bust out a quick dance party while the coffee brews.

It's Friday, baby, and that means a trip to Trader Joe's once I finish my lap around the trail! I pry open the space between my phone and its case to slip my credit card in and head out the door. I'm too insecure about my finances to use real money at the grocery store. This is not the first time in my adult life I've put food on credit. I don't like it, but it's where I'm at.

I've been broke before—zeros in the bank and a credit card balance. There are too many parallels to my life now that I can feel the anxiety rise despite my tranquil surroundings. I've reached the part of the trail where I'm basically at the water level, and it's serene as fuck. The river is a reflective mirror of the sky, and the sunshine through the bright green leaves of spring is delightful.

I'm not broke. I'm not under the double yellow line separating me from labeling my venture as a failure. That's a hard label to peel off. Too many small businesses have suffered this year, and many have crossed the double yellow line. I don't have a magic formula or potion that will protect me. I have a little money. Thankfully, my business expenses have evaporated like the travel industry, which makes me sad to think about.

I felt so special breezing into the airport lounges. They are a pleasure I could never take for granted. All it took was a $595 annual fee and a ticket to somewhere. Oh, and a reason. Sometimes I made them up like when Edward, my darling ex, suggested I go to D.C. back in December. I was a member of that special lounge club for ten whole weeks.

Let's be real here, I was just using every perk to the extreme. I ate meals there, I used the lotion in the bathroom, I'd take an Americano to go… I even managed to get a single free manicure at the Centurion Lounge in Miami. It was really pretty, and I snapped a photo and sent it to my boyfriend at the time, Andrew. The way he spoke about the massages and manicures in some Centurion Lounges had a mythical vibe. I was hell-bent on taking advantage of this opportunity as soon as I could travel again!

Oh, the glory days. I was blessed with another video WhatsApp call from my friend Kyle yesterday. He told me he knew COVID-19 was going to be a big deal when the airport lounges closed. To this day I didn't realize they were closed, but of course they are. I guess I thought that world was carrying on without me.

CHAPTER 3

TONY!

———

It's only after we've lost everything that we're free to do anything.
—CHUCK PALAHNIUK

October 16, 2019

Victory lap time! We just finished our third, and final, day at the Association of the United States Army's (AUSA) annual conference. The team is out of steam, but we rocked it. Every goal we set, we met. My team is awesome!

At this hour, the convention floor of the Walter E. Washington Convention Center in D.C. is beginning to thin out. Most folks are heading to their hotels to get fancy for the black-tie event tonight. The large conference booths, seemingly sold by the acre, are still lit to show off the latest big, angry military equipment. I've become desensitized to the next-generation war machines and looking straight down the barrel of weapons. They're much less threatening today. Perhaps this is due to the showroom-floor shine and new tank smell. It's hard to say.

I'm here wearing multiple hats, like many people. As the project manager of a contract team—read: not government civilians or military personnel—I keep our team on task and well-caffeinated. As a strategic communications professional, I make sure the speakers from AFC have what they need.

It has been a long three days, but we're pretty much finished. Craig, a guy from my team, pops his head in the little room I've landed in inside our booth and asks me if we can talk. It's a general rule in government contracting to not talk about the client in front of the client, so I pull myself out of the chair and follow him out onto the convention floor. We walk past the air, land, and sea warfare booths on our way out to the foyer. I'm eye-level with something canon-like that would look more at home on top of rubble. I would also look more at home somewhere else. Never thought I'd have much in common with a… what is this? The sign above me says I'm at the BAE Systems booth and my new steel friend is called an Extended Range Cannon Artillery (ERCA). Yep. Someone named that correctly.

Craig and I pulled over to take a snack break in the main foyer and found an empty table. It was sticky from all the snackers who'd come before—disgusting conference heathens. Craig was advocating for a raise, and I was trying to stay engaged in the conversation. It was not the best timing, and I was not endowed with the authority to give the man a Coke, let alone a raise.

As if on cue, my phone starts buzzing, and I look down to see who's calling. It's Gary, our corporate manager. I tried to perk up my voice and answered, "Hey Gary." I know, not a perky start.

"Julie, how are you." It was a statement not a question.

"I'm sitting here with Craig. We just wrapped up the last thing for AUSA and are taking a snack break. How are you?" "I'm okay." Pause. "Hey, don't react…"

That's the best line ever! Nothing says "great news" like telling someone not to react. Someone should write a blog post on phrases managers may want to avoid using. Suggested title: Three Ways to Emotionally Hijack Your Employees!

I sat still and tried not to convey to Craig, waiting to continue advocating for a salary bump, that I am getting demoted just as we limp over the finish line at AUSA. Let me clarify: me, Julie, is not getting demoted. The position I occupy on the organizational (org) chart is.

"Gary, can we talk about this tomorrow? I have ten minutes before I'm supposed to huddle with General Murray's team to discuss coverage of the Secretary of the Army's (SecArmy) upcoming visit." General Murray is a four-star general and is also known as the Commanding General (CG), the boss (said internally), the big boss (said externally), or Sir (said with a quick head nod). He is never without his two 24/7 ride-or-die guys. One, his executive officer, is a colonel and the other, his aide-de camp, is a captain. They are simultaneously detached and all-knowing. I'm forever fascinated by this balance.

If you're looking for more details on the conversation with Gary, I'm not the one to go to. I stopped listening after I got the message: the client (AFC) does not want a project manager on our contract and are downgrading that position, the one I currently occupy, effective whenever they made that change, could have been last week for all I know.

I advocated months ago for the client to restructure the team with a real project manager. One of those credentialed certified project management professional (PMP) types would be grand. This way my brain could return to doing what it does best. At the time, that was setting CSM Crosby up for success. The command team is made up of only two people: the CG and the CSM. It's a 51/49 split. The CSM is the senior enlisted person in the organization, and CSM Crosby was rolling around on the rubble in Syria before coming to AFC. There is nothing in between. One day you're in a war zone, and the next day you're at a flag ceremony in Austin. The resilience of people at his level blows my mind.

This little org chart action is nowhere near as extreme as going from Syria to Austin, but it's definitely not what I advocated for. What just happened is a scalpel on a document that won't save Uncle Sam a dime but will cost all of us more time and cause confusion. The project manager has the authority to do paperwork like vacation and overtime, and they assign personnel to work on tasks the government sends our way. It's not real authority, but if your organization is top heavy and there is no buffer between taskers and taskees, it's gonna get weird. Introducing "weird" in a military hierarchy is not recommended.

Thankfully, I'm getting better at meditating. I visualized duct taping my emotions so they couldn't scream and shoving them into the trunk of a nineties Buick. My buddha is a little Italian mobster named Tony who currently lives in New Jersey. I left Craig and found the room with the CG's ride-or-die guys. If you've ever been to a large conference, you know how easy it is to find a conversation in-progress when the eight-foot-tall walls are made of plastic and rattle when touched. The operational security (OPSEC) is lacking.

The topic of this meeting is a VIP visit. The SecArmy is coming to Austin, and somehow the girl currently endowed with no authority to be here is the one in the room. Where were the Public Affairs Office (PAO) folks? Or the Colonel or any one of his civilians? Where's the guy with the scalpel? Shrug emoji.

The duct tape held, and I was able to contribute to the meeting. I suggested Travis, our ridiculously talented videographer, do the thing that he loves: be creative and deliver something we can post on social media. He had just produced daily videos at AUSA, and I figured he'd be game for more overtime.

This conference is the first time anyone on our contract team has received overtime. Why not keep going? The paperwork can be amended, and we need the varsity all-star for a SecArmy visit.

I stayed behind to do the paperwork, and that's when it hit me. This is not my job anymore. I don't have the authority to do this. Oof. "Keep doing what you're doing, Julie," was how Gary ended our call. If you're savvy on government contracting, you know it's not okay to downgrade a position and expect the same scope of work. If you went into this paragraph not savvy, at least now you know why I'm upset.

I can feel the duct tape failing. I close my eyes, inhale, and summon Tony, visualizing him opening the trunk, punching my emotions, and slamming the lid back down.

Do not cry.

Just get out... get out... finish the day and get back to the beautiful Mayflower Hotel. My darling ex-boyfriend, Edward, Ubered me there a few years ago to meet his friends. A couple months after we broke up, one of those guys was publicly ejected from his position at the White House. D.C. is such a small town. If you buy me a slice of cake, I'll tell you who. (Kidding, that gossip will cost you the whole cake.)

When my team was tasked with supporting AFC at AUSA, I started searching for a Marriott hotel within a decent radius of the convention center. All the close ones were booked up once AUSA announced the dates last year. This is an industry known for planning and preparation, and they're very good at execution. I went with the Mayflower. I'd only been back to the bar one other time to cheer up a friend. She'd sent me a text saying she just saw wedding photos of her ex-boyfriend on Facebook. Cue the full perk-up package: a drink, dessert, and some old money luxury. The Mayflower didn't disappoint.

I had dinner plans with a work friend and was looking forward to talking about anything other than work. The sooner I'm surrounded by civility, the better. Sometimes the cure for feeling shitty is as simple as having someone bring me food. Sometimes the situation calls for a proper napkin. I think busting my ass for three days to make my client look good and then learning I've been demoted counts. I know better than to take an org chart personally, but it doesn't make this any less shitty. Thankfully, I had plans at an establishment with proper napkins.

Everything was going to be okay.

* * *

It was not okay. Nope. Not okay.

We were still in the Uber on the way to the restaurant when my dinner companion decided to tell me one of my colleagues had said to, "Be careful with Julie."

I inhale.

One good thing about finding out you've been dripping blood from the knife in your back is that you can see the trail.

There is no wondering how things will play out or what she meant by that specifically. The show is over. Damage done. I exhale.

Another good thing is getting to fly to Austin tomorrow, and I'll be back on a plane on Sunday to spend nine days in California. I'm out of good things. Two feels like a lot to come up with right now.

* * *

Apparently, Tony didn't make the trip to California. Once I get to Palm Springs, the duct tape rips off and my emotions escape the trunk like a scene from *Breaking Bad*. Well, if *Breaking Bad* was set in the desert outside the luxurious JW Marriott Hotel. It has three restaurants—all with proper napkins—and the valet removed my emotions from the trunk of that rental car and hung them neatly in the closet with my luggage.

You know when adults who've been through some shit talk about "doing the work?" I'm no adult, but I did go through that closet and tried on all the emotions. I felt the feels.

The way the org chart changes were handled makes me angry and sad, disappointed and embarrassed, and... over it. I want to be done here. AFC is not the place I thought it was going to be. I thought the headquarters would be the center of the solar system, but Pluto is the one making innovation happen. Organizationally, Pluto represents all the bottom squirkles (that's a real word for rounded-corner squares, and we can all thank Travis for teaching me this) on the org chart. That's where the researchers and soldiers are. Human capital and legal are at headquarters.

I wanted to be out on Pluto, or at least on one of Saturn's rings—somewhere on the edge! Instead, I'm at a five-star resort complaining that it's not Pluto. I'm ridiculous.

Ann, a dear, dear friend, is here for back-to-back conferences, and I am sleeping in the other queen bed. Ann invited me to come on her work trip and telework, since it was in Cali-for-ni-YAY. We planned this back in May, and I went into AUSA knowing I could depend on California as time to rest and recover. After AUSA last year, I foolishly went to the office the next day—which is not recommended. So, when the opportunity came to fly away and spend nine days in gorgeous Marriott hotels on someone else's dime, I jumped on it!

The JW transformed into my convalescent home. I did the work, so Tony didn't have to. I was frustrated I wouldn't be transitioning to support the CSM, someone I respect and admire. I was also frustrated someone felt people needed to be careful of me. The thing that bothered me the most, though, is that I don't know what to do next. I can hear Tony's slick-haired old guy Jersey accent offering to "take care of it" for me, but I can't hear my gut. Without my intuition, I don't know what's next.

Eventually, Palm Springs ended, and we had to leave for San Diego—where Ann's second conference is located. Before we leave, I pause on a rattan loveseat in the shade to call my client. I rehearsed my part of the conversation and knew it would be best if I didn't take the feeling, I should call him, with me to San Diego. I told him exactly what I've told you—the conversation with Gary, the hearsay, and how I don't know what my role is now. He was not surprised. He reiterated we were one team, and each had value to add. He told me he wanted me to work on special projects with him, starting with one he was pulling together for the CG now. He would work on it over the weekend and send it to me.

Over the next week I sent three follow-up emails about that project, offering my help. He never gave the opportunity.

* * *

Ann drove us to the lovely Marriott Marquis on the water, and we unpacked for another few days. She keeps a tidy hotel room. I do not. If left unchecked, I can destroy a hotel room like the tiger in *The Hangover*. We sang our hearts out on the drive to San Diego. A classic nineties Hollywood road trip cliche all the way.

Ann morphed back into conference vendor mode, and I played tourist. It was the weekend, after all. I did as many things as Google could suggest. I went to the zoo. I rented a bike on Catalina Island. I saw the seals in La Jolla. I visited coffee shops and putzed around. I ate a lot of fish in restaurants. I had breakfast at the fancy-pants lounge at the hotel because Ann is in the cool kids' club. Hotel breakfast is my favorite thing in the whole wide world, but breakfast in a fancy-pants lounge is on a whole other level. Literally.

After a nice putz around downtown and buying chocolate at one of the many shops, I decided to stop at the Chinese History Museum. The docent suggested I purchase entrance to both museums, which was news to me because I just stumbled onto this one. It only cost seven dollars for both, so why not?

The docent was a sweetheart. I was the only one in there, so she went through each display with great care. The museum had a beautiful collection of items Chinese immigrants brought with them to the United States, and dioramas explaining what their lives were like. Eventually, she sent me out the door to the second museum. It's catty-corner from the original. This gave me a chance to pop another chocolate in my mouth. I didn't dare eat inside. She was librarian-level serious, so I figured chocolate sampling was bad form.

The kid at the other museum did not give a flying fruit basket that I was there. He let me wander and read at my leisure. He didn't care that I took photos. The collection was on dragons, and I was sucked in by their mystique.

Somewhere inside the museum, I decide I'm going to start my own company. Instead of helping the Army communicate to the defense innovation community, I could help those companies communicate with the entire military. I was going to need a mascot or logo. Hello dragon! I walked in with a sugar-free salted caramel in my mouth and walked out breathing fire. It's one of those experiences you half expect to be a weird dream. Like, if I tried to find the museum today someone would tell me "It burned down back in 1875…"

Who cares? I'm getting off this org chart, and I'm adopting a dragon.

* * *

Why make my own org chart and not just go back to D.C. and find another contracting gig?

Two reasons: number one, I don't want to leave the mission, and number two, I'm tired of playing that game.

Those lead to better questions, right? Like, what mission? Why don't you want to leave it? Aren't there other missions? And what game?

The answers involve unzipping my chest and showing you the deep dark scars. Skip to the sixth chapter if you don't want to see inside of there.

CHAPTER 4

THE VETERAN

Love, always.

—DAD

Once upon a time, in an airport far, far away...

My adorable six-year-old self is walking through some airport with my father. Fat cheeks, blonde curls, and a happy demeanor: that's me, not my dad.

My parents divorced when I was four, and after a couple years my father got a job at a university far, far away. As kids, my two siblings and I flew as unaccompanied minors when we visited. We went every summer and every other winter. Flying unaccompanied had a profoundly influential impact on me. It was magical to feel the adventure and independence. To this day, I love airports and planes. I don't care if I'm in the middle seat because that's where I usually was—between my older brother and sister.

I have no idea why there was an American soldier in this airport. This was in the late eighties, and I remember my father looking at the guy and saying, "Good morning Staff Sergeant, how are you today?" And you know what? The guy made eye contact with my father and answered. Seriously, that's the whole story. So, my father said hello to a guy in uniform—big deal, right?! Yeah. Big deal.

My father, who enlisted in the Air Force during Vietnam, demonstrated how important it is to address members of the military with their rank. In the moments that passed after the simple exchange with that soldier, I learned more about military culture than I learned during my twenties as an Army spouse. He explained that staff sergeants have been in the military long enough to have seen some things. According to my father, those things were things I couldn't imagine—so mysterious! As a six-year-old, he was probably right.

With a quick glance from this guy's chest to his eyes, my father communicated to him he could see him, and he honored him. It's a language that veterans speak, and it connects them like a secret code. Few civilians know how many chevrons and semi-circle things add up to a lifetime of service. That moment stayed with me. I can spot a staff sergeant, but my morning greeting doesn't connect the way it would from a fellow veteran.

When my siblings and I boarded those planes and hopped from the West Coast to the middle of nowhere USA, we would literally swap lives with our stepsister. My sister and I would sleep in her bed, hang our clothes in her closet, and use her shampoo. The norm, at the time, was not to integrate step-kids if they didn't need to live in the same house together. One trip to the airport and my father could drop off my stepsister and return home with three different children.

Rebecca, my stepsister, had a waterbed, which is only relevant because if you've slept next to someone in a waterbed, then you know how the two of you become one—not in a creepy way, but in a "don't rock the boat" way. This bonded my sister and I even more than the divorce had. The waterbed was the stage where my father's bedtime stories were told. He would make his rounds between my brother's room across the hall and where we were. He'd tuck us in and tell one wild tale after another.

Eventually, he would leave to do whatever adults do when children are in bed, which I imagine involves eating cookies. My sister and I would lay silently in the dark until finally one of us would say, "What was he talking about?"

My father treated his time with us as a limited opportunity to impart as much wisdom as he could. So, bedtime stories were his chance to teach us how the world worked. There were cyanide capsules, tips on where to hide a passport in a hotel room, lessons on how to know if your room had been searched, etc. The backdrop was the Soviet Union during the Cold War. A year ago, I shared some of these stories with a friend at the State Department.

"Do you think he was a spy?" he asked.

"Nope."

A few moments went by and I asked, "Wait, a spy for us or for Russia?" Neither of us answered.

Part of my upbringing was shaped by stories of the hero hiding cash in the toilet tank. When I was a kid, it seemed weird. But fast-forward twenty-five years, and I'm in North Africa in "hotel jail"—funny how it doesn't faze me. I wasn't allowed to leave the hotel until the next morning when the embassy driver pulled up past the checkpoint with the bomb sniffing dog and swept the car with some electronic contraption. Why? I wasn't safe. Cyanide capsules somehow don't seem all that out of place anymore.

That peek into my chest wasn't so bad, was it? There's one more scar you should see, and then it'll all make sense.

CHAPTER 5

THE BOMB

———

Before the bomb hits, there comes a shriek that splits your soul.
—BARBARA NICKLESS

I don't know much about bombs, but I know one kind very, very well. You're familiar with those spy thriller movies, right? The villain, an evil and gloriously good-looking man, hides a bomb in some high-trafficked spot. He sets the timer to go off at the worst possible time. Then, he disappears in a puff of smoke.

Right?

That happened to me, metaphorically.

Much like the plot of every James Bond movie I've seen, the bomb was placed there by an evil villain. Honestly, I don't think the man playing the villain here knew the extent of the damage he could cause.

I was attacked ten years ago. I'm a woman in my late thirties, so statistically, we all know it's probably not the only time. It's the only time I kept a secret, though.

By keeping it quiet, I thought I'd be better off. So, when I heard the bomb tick, which happened a few times a year,

I would try my best to muffle the sound. Something would trigger it and I'd be emotionally hijacked. This is how I learned to duct tape my emotions until I could be alone with them. It took all my concentration to keep up the facade that everything was fine. I knew my breath was shaky. I knew I had an hour, maybe two, before I fell apart. Privately, of course. What good is a secret if you can't keep it hidden?

The night I met Hal, back in 2018, was my first time at the Embassy of Afghanistan in D.C. Don't hate Hal, he's the hero of this story, even if I curse him at the end.

I was lucky enough to bump into the 6'4" Hal. A tree of a human. He had that leftover special forces scruffy beard thing going on that's just adorable. I don't remember how it started, but we chatted for a minute in the hallway before he broke off. A little while later he popped up at the table I was at, trying to make conversation with a man who couldn't figure out if I was worth his time, and I looked up and met his kind eyes. "You again," I said. Smiling he responded, "Me again."

That became our greeting, and it never failed to give me that butterfly feeling. I'd see his name pop up on my phone and I'd answer with, "You again." And I'd hear, "Me again." It was absolutely fucking adorable for as long as it lasted. Also, shoutout to Hal for using his phone to make actual calls.

I struggled in D.C. to feel like I had any credibility. It's a tough town, and I never felt like I arrived. I tried to find a way to be taken seriously, to operate there and get the right stamp on my passport. It's not an easy place for women to establish intellectual credibility. The six years I spent in D.C. were rough. I showed up there as an unpaid intern at thirty-one-years-old. I went from making zero to mid-six figures in six years.

I had to make up for lost time, and I had no intention of being lax about it. Also, I'd always wanted to operate in the international space. I wanted to be there more from a place of professional curiosity than as a subject matter expert. If I'm honest here, I never found a subject that could hold my attention long enough to build the foundation I'd need to stand my ground around the intellectuals and experienced elite in Washington.

It was a struggle to find my identity there and be comfortable in it. I wasn't prepared to simultaneously figure out who I was and compete with the people who seemed to have life figured out. Washington is not a safe place to take a risk. The exception is politics because politicians don't fail; they lose. Big banks and government bailouts, too, don't fail; they take heavy losses. Some folks land on their feet in Washington—some folk like Hal. That's simply how it works.

I had just started a nonprofit—my now failed nonprofit. (How do you fail at a nonprofit? By making a profit? Ha! No, you just don't win any grants and move on with your life.) It's refreshing to say because now that I live in Austin, there's a completely different feeling. You're allowed to fail here and expected to have failed! How else will you have learned anything? When people ask me if I like living in Austin, the answer they get comes out with a gush. "Oh, I love Austin and what it's done for me." If anyone asks the obvious follow-up question, I get the opportunity to tell them it has given me the freedom to fuck up.

Hal walked with a lifetime of credibility in every step. He had been a special forces weapons sergeant and earned the right to consider himself hot shit. I put him on a pedestal, and he looked like Michelangelo's David up there.

"Let me know when you're ready to go, I'll walk out with you," he said after overhearing me tell two guys I would not be joining them for drinks after. The boy scout was looking out for me. I took him up on his offer and when we got outside, I pulled out my phone to order an Uber. "Not to be creepy, but that's my truck right there. I could just take you home."

Well played, Hal. Well played.

I took a deep breath, weighed my options, and decided I wanted more time with this man. Sure, I had him pull into the wrong parking lot at my condo, and I walked to the wrong entrance. If he was going to stalk me, he was going to have to put a little work in.

We started dating as I was going through a massive transition. I was on a contract at the DOD IG, and it was coming to an end. I was on site to be the nice guy who guilted them into continuing it for a few more months.

Everyone at work knew the contract was ending. However, they didn't know I had no intention of staying with the company nor that I wanted to be off on my own.

A month or two into our relationship, Hal went on vacation to climb Kilimanjaro. You know how these guys are, right? Then, he putzed around a bit in some other places. Again, just doing life the way these guys do. I was working on trying to get a proposal approved by a company in D.C. to do some communications and public relations work when suddenly, it fell apart. My plan B was to take the job at Army Futures Command as a Senior Communications Specialist making really good money. On paper, plan B did not suck.

When my ex-husband and I divorced, he got the Army. It wasn't written in the decree, but it was his career. That was his branch—his agency, not mine. It's bad enough I fall head over heels for these guys, isn't it? Do I really have to work with them, too? With Hal overseas, I decided I needed to pop out of town before getting locked up in another contract. I negotiated a start date two weeks away and began to plan my escape. Hal was near the summit when I decided to go to Colombia. We didn't even talk about it until I was in Cartagena and he was down the other side of the mountain.

Like a good boy scout, he picked me up from the airport. On the way to his place he gently suggested I consider getting a device when I travel so people know where I am. He tried to fill the silence in the truck that followed with, "My brother and I do it with each other, it just helps everyone know someone is looking out for them."

"You want me to wear a PTL?" That was my only reply. It was more of a statement than a question. I was a contractor at the State Department long enough to know what a personnel tracking locator (PTL) was. Think of them as portable devices you keep with you so the government knows where you are. What was that? You say it sounds a lot like a cell phone? Pretty much.

I knew what procedural tripwires had to be triggered before they were issued. Issuing a PTL implies a lack of safety or security. I was unwilling to entertain the thought that my ability to handle myself overseas warranted carrying a PTL.

We all know he was right, and there have been many times where it would be nice to think someone knew where I was. But there was something in his gentle request that ticked me off. Sometimes these guys think they're the only ones who can take care of themselves. Sometimes they're right. But sometimes, they're sheepdogs who exist to take care of the rest of us. Hal was both.

I came back from that trip, spent the night at Hal's, and was back out the door to catch a 3:00 a.m. train from D.C. to N.Y.C. to attend Concordia. A friend had an extra ticket. They're hundreds, if not thousands, of dollars.

Concordia is non-profit prom. World leaders are in town for the UN General Assembly, and they make an appearance at Concordia. It's a small gathering that feels even more intimate with the fancy badge for VIP access. I'm a lucky girl!

I was on top of the world—ready to bring world peace to the masses.

In exchange for delaying my start date on the contract at Army Futures Command to accommodate the trip to Colombia and Concordia, I offered to work AUSA 2018. There were a few short weeks of in-processing between getting back from my adventure and the conference. Maybe if I'd had more time to ramp up and find my groove, I would have handled it better.

Spoiler: I did not handle it well at all.

The first day at AUSA was a firehose. I think I cried that night, but I don't remember. The second night, though, the bomb in my chest exploded. I didn't know how to handle the death and destruction on display at the conference. I was uncomfortable with the show of force—of all the money spent to kill people.

I'm still uncomfortable. I know my heart is with the mission to modernize the military, because I'm in it for the warfighter, not for war. I've loved them. I've adored them. I respect them. From my high school sweetheart to my most recent ex-boyfriend, I can't fight the instinct that makes me want to dedicate my life to bringing them home, because it's stronger than I am.

I left the second day overwhelmed by the war machine. I went to a Devex event at George Washington University that evening. Devex is a media platform that hosts business development-type events for the global development community. I foolishly thought I could support both: humanitarians and warfighters.

I was wrong. I wept in the dark auditorium at Devex. I couldn't reconcile the nonprofit leaders talking about how little they needed to make a big difference with the day I'd had. I'd climbed into a tank earlier worth more than they'd ever ask for. I pretended to pilot an Osprey, too. Because I could.

So, I let the tears fall.

When it was over and I'd wiped my face, I saw how many missed calls and texts I had from Hal. I put my order in for an Uber home and called him back. There was never any option to fake a happy voice with Hal. He always knew.

I tried to keep it short and just tell him I was tired. I had a breakfast event in the morning, and it would be best to take a shower and pull myself together for the final conference day. He didn't like it, but he let me off the hook as long as I called him before bed.

* * *

Have you pieced it together yet that my attacker wore an Army uniform? When we install the kill switch in our warfighters, we don't install an off switch. For some people, you never know they're capable of war. For others, you can see the monster in their eyes. One night many years ago I met the monster. I tried to forget, but my body couldn't.

I got out of the Uber and into my condo. The second blast had gone off in my chest and I was searching for somewhere to cry. I found a safe place curled on the floor of the bathtub. It's remarkably soothing with the shower running.

The whiplash between war and peace—between AUSA and Concordia/Devex—let the ticking in my chest go too far. I wish I could tell you time heals all wounds, but it doesn't. Sometimes wounds don't heal by themselves.

"Nope, nope, nope, I'm okay. You don't need to come over." Poor guy would have done anything to make the pain go away. I told him about the monster that haunted me and the bomb in my chest. He understood because he'd known many monsters and seen more than his share of bombs go off, literally and figuratively.

Being at AUSA, seeing all that war, and knowing I was an active participant now in making more monsters was a trigger for trauma.

Hal very kindly gave me a nudge to find help. He made valid points about how I had a steady income, health insurance, and a really good support system of friends and family. Basically, I had everything I could ever want to become my own bomb squad and defuse it.

Bless him for that. This is the reason I met Hal. Two weeks later, I talked to a friend, a military intelligence officer, about it.

"He's right, but I don't know who I'd talk to."

"I do," she said.

Just like that. Like, "Hey if you're serious about defusing this bomb, I know a guy."

She did. Now I do, too. Timeout for a shoutout: if you need help or know someone who does, assistance is available from Headstrong. It's free for veterans and the occasional Julie.

The trauma therapy connected me on a personal level to the world of defense innovation (the use of innovative tools and techniques for the purpose of ensuring our warfighters can be effective and efficient). It included a modality called eye movement desensitization and reprocessing (EMDR). EMDR is amazing. The first session with my therapist was just chatting. The second session we did EMDR in a soft way. The third session we got into it.

EMDR works by reprogramming the brain and covering triggers with pleasant memories. In psychology speak, information related to stressful events is sometimes ineffectively processed. EMDR works by stimulating the brain to process and heal memories, ultimately linking them to positive memory networks.[1]

Twelve hours after the third session, I was vomiting. I threw up all night. It was an exorcism.

I didn't see the connection until my dear, dear friend Ann pointed it out. I'd sent her a text that I'd thrown up, because I hardly ever puke, and her response was painfully simple.

"Didn't you get sick the last time you saw your therapist?"

What the… Oh my god, she's right. I did. I didn't puke, but I was nauseous that night in bed.

OK, now we know what's happening. Ten years of pent up trauma is leaving my body. On the bathroom floor, I typed out an email to my therapist. I also emailed the office and told them I was sick. One of my coworkers wrote back, "don't get us sick."

I let out a sigh.

---

1   Jason N. Linder, PsyD, "What the Heck is EMDR Therapy? Can It Really Help Me?" Psychology Today, July 19, 2020."

My therapist had me come in that morning and we did the protocol in a softer, more healing way. I haven't heard the ticking in my chest since.

Dear Hal,

Angel, thank you. I swear, I didn't mean all the horrible things I said about you that night on the bathroom floor.

Love,

Julie

* * *

The reason Hal was in my life, and the reason I thought you needed to see the deep, dark bits inside of me is because it shows you the setpoint of bullshit I'm willing to work with. The mission is stronger than anything else. I couldn't have stayed with the contract at Army Futures Command if it wasn't. I wouldn't have moved to Austin for it. I certainly wouldn't have cried frustrated tears in front of the CSM about it.

I wouldn't still be on this journey without it. You see, none of the bullshit or the frustration can ever be worse than walking around holding a ticking time bomb for ten years.

My alignment, my purpose, my Simon Sinek "why"—my whatever—is the warfighter. (Because they're dying, remember?) I've cared about them and loved a handful. They're why I'm with it. I love my country, democracy, freedom, and capitalism—all of the American ideals. But I love the warfighter more. They show up to do the job I wasn't willing to do myself.

CHAPTER 6

MEET MR. WONDERFUL

———

Some of the best things that have ever happened to us wouldn't have happened to us, if it weren't for some of the worst things that have ever happened to us.

—MOKOKOMA MOKHONOANA

The night Mr. Wonderful asked for my number was after a local AUSA chapter event on November 24, 2019. AUSA hosted a meet and greet at Capital Factory, and there are many things I could tell you about the event. But I'm going to focus on three: Capital Factory, free food, and Andrew.

First, Capital Factory is a tech-bro WeWork-esque coworking destination in Austin. They are heavily involved, and invested, in defense innovation (a.k.a. military modernization). Capital Factory was part of the tour when the Army went on a multi-city house-hunting trip for AFC's HQ, and they're even more invested in the ecosystem today. The Army Applications Laboratory (AAL), AFC's cool kids club, is located on the eighth floor, and all the big defense companies have membership at Capital Factory so they can keep an eye on things.

Second, there is the free food! I can almost always graze through the day at Capital Factory. On this night we had a fajita/taco bar. I remember because it was the first time I'd chatted with one of the few women at AFC, and we bonded over our shared keto plates. The gender mix at this event mirrors the industry, as in I can recall only four of us women out of the one hundred guests, and she and I discussed it briefly. We also discussed our lack of interest in men in Austin. When you're accustomed to the dashing and dangerous types of D.C., a hipster looks like a child. Of course, there were a few dashing and dangerous men at AFC HQ, but they were married, and also, we work there. There is one eligible bachelor, however, who happened to be standing on the other side of the room. I may have mentioned Andrew's existence, or perhaps she did, but I know he came up.

Third, I toss my empty plate with remnants of fajita chicken and guacamole and went over to say hello to Andrew. Not necessarily to flirt, but because he's always nice and not creepy. In a room full of men, it's good to know who your allies are.

"Hey," he greeted me with his beautiful smile.

"Hi."

"You should have come by sooner. We're just heading out to salsa dancing at the W Hotel. You should come."

"Oh, I've never been. Maybe." We smile and part ways. Poor timing, but interesting.

At this point, I'd been nice to strangers for twelve hours and had nothing left. On my walk home I was passing the W and figured it wouldn't hurt to stop. It is 8:13 p.m. Come on Jules, have a bit of fun!

Andrew was nowhere to be found. They have a secret red room (um, YEAH) with a bar, and the nice lady at the door escorted me in. She was in no rush because the place was empty.

Almost. There was one suit drinking alone. That suit was the man holding the org chart scalpel and too much power over my life. Thanks to this guy, it's also the day I had to tell two of my colleagues their jobs were ending, and their services would no longer be required once the ball drops in Times Square. Happy Thanksgiving. Merry Christmas. Good luck out there.

I had a choice. I could walk into the red room and talk to him, or I could spin on my heel and walk out. I was already making plans to leave AFC at the end of the year, so I had nothing to lose. *Naive little girl.*

Folks, I don't want to tell you what happened next, but I think it's for your benefit; it's not for mine, that's for sure. At the end of the night, Andrew walked me home and asked me to join him for dinner the next evening—the night he'd be crowned Mr. Wonderful. So, that part of the story ends well. But before that happened, the suit got drunk, put his hand on my leg, and called me "babe." More than once.

AUTHOR'S NOTE

I don't want this in the book because I am embarrassed and ashamed. I didn't explode. I didn't break his hand. I didn't choke him. I didn't do the things people like to say they would do in that situation. Why? A few reasons:

1. This kind of shit happens every day. I know how this story plays out if I do anything other than try to mitigate the damage he is responsible for. Spoiler: the contractor always loses.

2. He still holds the scalpel.

3. In my experience, when men with power are embarrassed, they're unpredictable.

4. Our boss is the one I called when I was in Palm Springs who had barely spoken to me since. I was without an ally.

So, I just watched the show and tried to manage the risk. Either he wouldn't remember, or he'd be too embarrassed to face me. He called in sick the next day, a Friday, and we never spoke about it.

Of all the stories I could put in here or leave out, why share this one? Because it matters, it happens all the time in this industry, and it's not okay. Not the way I behaved, or didn't, or the way he did, or didn't. We all know what right looks like, and this ain't it. It's just me and you here, so let's be honest. It's not like you'll do anything about it either.

* * *

Text December 21, 2019 9:11 a.m.

Me: So… I've got a potential client looking to build meaningful relationships globally with the local governments. I'm hunting paths that are more concrete than the grant programs at State.

Thoughts?

That's how it begins. I'm out on a romantic weekend with Andrew and texting my darling ex, Edward. Andrew took me to a posh treehouse a few hours away from Austin. It was on his bucket list, and it conveniently fell into the only item on my list: random awesome adventures. So, here we are up in a treehouse finishing a breakfast of yogurt parfaits and copious cups of coffee. Okay fine, he's drinking coffee like a normal person and I'm drinking it like I've found the fountain of youth.

I don't want you to think I'm a floozy. I'm totally committed to Mr. Wonderful. Our first date was a magical evening that left me floating. As soon as I got home and settled, I sent a text to some girlfriends saying I had just returned home from a date with Mr. Wonderful. Then, I put the phone down and went to bed. In the morning, the replies didn't ask for Mr. Wonderful's identity, they were astonished I'd been on a date.

Me, too. I like my drama-free life with no wondering if a man will text me or let me down. (I know, there should be more between those two, but there isn't.) This one, though, this Mr. Wonderful might just be wonderful.

We explored Podunkville, the closest town to the treehouse, and found a little antique store. Among the knick-knacks, he innocently asked me where my desk would be.

"I don't know? I have global WeWork access with my AmEx so I can go anywhere. I think there are four or five within walking distance of my apartment. I'll sample." I'd been working at one of them, so I knew what to expect.

Except, I didn't. That evening, while waiting for our beige small-town-America dinners to arrive, it hit me. I'm alone.

I made the universal "holy shit" face: frozen, wide-eyed, lots of blinking, staring at one spot, and lips ajar. Andrew, unaware anything had changed in the past ten seconds, slowly asked if I was ok.

"Oh. My. God." Another ten seconds passed, or two. I don't know.

"Did something bite you?" Andrew asked. A legit question in the only restaurant open for dinner in Podunkville. This is rural Texas, folks.

"I'm alone."

"No, I'm here." To his credit, he tried. I bet he was calculating how long would it take to pack up and drive back. Clearly the woman in front of him, his crowned "girlfriend" of three whole weeks, is not as connected to reality as he was led to believe.

"On January 1: DEFIANT. No one is coming with me. I mean, I have my team. But I'm the only one going to WeWork that day. I'll be alone."

I like hanging out with me. I'm cool. I just hadn't realized I was all by myself on January 1. Logically I knew I was the one setting up an LLC and separating from the traditional narrative (go to college, get a good job, marry someone, buy a house, make babies, etc,) again. I filled out the paperwork, filed it with the state of Texas, and paid the $300 fee for the LLC. I applied for the AmEx business platinum card. That was me.

I just didn't realize I was alone in this.

* * *

Text December 21, 2019 1:35 p.m.

Edward: Yes

Me: Are you going to share them?

Edward: We'll talk about it the next time you're in town.

Uh oh.

Me: You're gonna make me come all that way, huh?

Like I said, it's just business. It's just complicated because I dated interesting men in D.C. This one, my darling, darling ex, is better connected and more influential than others. He's also the reason I called my mother at 3:00 a.m. four years ago and made her tell me everything was going to be okay. This man broke me. I called in sick and spent the next day on Ann's sofa with my head in her lap watching *Big Bang Theory* while she petted my hair. I still love him, because love doesn't disappear.

However, as the unattributable Pinterest quote says, "a relit cigarette never tastes the same."

And I've only ever smoked cigars.

* * *

Some exes are better than others. This one has a two-bedroom over a metro station on the same line as Reagan National Airport (DCA). He also knows how the game is played better than I do.

Text December 26, 2019 2:14 p.m.

Me: Alright Mr. Mister... are you in town January 5... 6... 7... ish?

Edward: Should be, if not keys are at the counter in the lobby

Me: Awww. You're the best

Edward: I am!

My last day at AFC is December 31, 2019 and my business c-section is scheduled for 12:01 a.m. on January 1, 2020! Now, it's up to me to figure out how to make my first business trip worth my money. So, who do I know? Friends, obviously, I lived there for six years. But they're friends, and they'll understand because this is my first business trip, I've got to prioritize business.

Two friends, Catherine and Kyle, are small business owners. Seeing either or both of them would be amazing. Hmm… maybe I can get in touch with AUSA while I'm there and talk about the new event they're planning in Austin in June…

* * *

WhatsApp December 27, 2019 10:51 p.m.

Me: I'll be in D.C. Jan 6-9. Any chance you'll be there too?

Kyle: I will!!! See you then :)

Me: Wow! Really?

Me: I can't believe it!!!

Me: Ok. Breakfast on the 7th?

Strike while the iron's hot, girlie!

Kyle: I would offer you a place to stay, but I moved back to Maryland to help out at home until my Mom recovers.

Kyle: Yes!

Recovers? How big of an asshole am I? What should I know? Quick... improvise!

Me: You're too kind. I don't think I know what your Mom is recovering from... but I'm sure you'll tell me

Me: I'll send a calendar invite. Still on K street?

Kyle: Yes

Me: Any good spots? I can Google it

Me: I'm just so excited to catch you!

You should all meet Kyle. How do I describe Kyle to you? On a personal level, he's the only man on this planet I'd leave my imaginary six kids and adoring husband for if he professed his love. I'm not sure I'd pause to grab my purse on the way out the door.

Yep. I'll be in love with my idealized version of Kyle for the rest of my life. Burn hot little torch... burn hot! He founded a company doing predictive impact analysis with clients like Mercy Corps and CARE. Fuck me, he's amazing. He was driven to leave a positive mark on society after being held hostage and ransomed. Yep. He took an unimaginable situation and turned it into a company. Oh, my heart just stops when I think about him...

* * *

Text December 29, 2019 3:25 p.m.

Catherine: Hi there! Hope you had a great Christmas! Happy New Year!!!!

Me: I was just thinking of you the other day!

Me: Hi!

Me: Merry Christmas and Happy New Year!

Me: I'm going to D.C. for some work and have availability on the 8th

Me: ?? I'd love to see you

Stalker much?

Text December 29, 2019 5:58 p.m.

Catherine: I would love to see you too!

Catherine: January 8 looks open.

* * *

Text December 31, 2019 5:01 p.m.

Andrew: Officially unemployed yet?

Me: Yes. Yes, I am. Until midnight

Andrew: Whooooo hoooooo

Me: I bought DEFIANT some cupcakes and candles. Lol

Andrew: I like it! Happy Birthday.

Holy cow. We're adorable. The plan is to pick up giant crab legs and watch the fireworks off my balcony—romantic and chill. Classic Andrew.

Two big things happened that night. A lot of little things happened, too. For example, we ate one hundred dollars worth of crab legs and made a huge mess all over my dining room table. Making a mess with the right person feels like jumping in puddles with rain boots. It's fantastic. We stretched out on the white rug on my living room floor and listened to some of our favorite music and podcasts. When two nerds enjoy each other's company... lol!

I shared my takeaways from the two-hour intention setting yoga session I went to. I adore the instructors at my nearby Black Swan Yoga studio. Patsy and JJ led the workshop and started us off with a meditation on 2019. I branded it the "Year of Growth" in my journal. By the end of the class we were meditating on 2020. I branded it the "Year of Abundance." Yep. Lots of abundance. I now realize the importance of being specific when speaking with the universe.

While Andrew and I we were lying on the floor, like normal people in front of a perfectly comfortable sofa, my phone dinged every fifteen minutes or so. It was Randy. He and another friend were my branding team going into DEFIANT. We'd had several meetings, always prefaced by brunch, and they shot my promo videos. Don't remember seeing those?

Yeah... my first one was supposed to post on LinkedIn in the morning.

Except, it didn't happen. We were making last minute revisions, only making it worse. I was frustrated, our friend was moving on to celebrate New Year's Eve, and Randy felt terrible. Randy is the human embodiment of everything wonderful about golden retrievers. He's talented, kind, and the hardest worker in the government. Everyone takes Randy for granted and don't know they're doing it. He was my rock from the moment I got to Austin, and we became "Randy and Julie" (a.k.a. "Dad and Mom" to the team). Our failure to launch DEFIANT's brand was the first time we'd ever not come through for each other. It was incomprehensible that there was something we couldn't do as a team. Neither of us knew how to work through it, so we stepped back for the night. What else could we do?

This did not bolster my confidence as midnight approached. In fact, it was a solid reminder I'm raising this baby as a single parent. Those two have real jobs. I'm the only one who can keep this business alive. I'm the only one who can make it successful. I'm the only one who will. I'm the only one who will be there in the middle of the night when it wakes me up and can't go back to sleep. I'm alone.

DEFIANT will be here in three hours. Holy fucking shit, what have I done?

* * *

Earlier I told you two things happened on New Year's Eve. The first was that we failed as a team. The second was that my baby was born. I'm thirty-eight years old, folks. This is what having a baby looks like at thirty-eight when you're divorced, single-ish (I know, Andrew… but it's not the same thing), and not participating in the traditional narrative.

No one throws you a business baby shower—no tiny onesies, soft animal books, crib sheets, and casserole deliveries. No diaper cake.

But, when my baby was born, there were cupcakes. The Whole Foods bakery section across from my apartment just happens to sell a four-pack of low-carb, low-sugar devil's food cupcakes. Boom. Added to cart.

I stood in front of the small candle section debating if I "needed" candles. The only ones on sale at Whole Foods, a place where even birthday cake candles were made of soy and non-toxic food dye, were as tall as the cupcakes. They were as expensive as the cupcakes, too.

If I "need" candles, in the first-world sense, what kind of candles? I can't just get one because it would be weird to have one cupcake with a candle when two people were sharing the experience. That move works on real cakes, but not on cupcakes. I finally settle on a zero and a one in fetchingly edible blue.

The second significant moment of New Year's Eve was when I picked up one cupcake in each hand and gave a toast. Candles burned on the top of each: a zero and a one. I recited the quote I committed to memory during the first act of *Hadestown* when I'd visited Manhattan three weeks ago. Ann and I met up to see the musical, walk the Highline, eat delicious food, shop the iconic Christmas markets, see the Rockefeller tree, watch the skaters below, have brunch in Brooklyn, and just enjoy life.

Early in the show, there is a line so beautiful I had to quickly stick it in my memory and hope it stayed there until intermission so I could type it into my phone. It was a simple two-line toast. Don't forget... don't forget...

Andrew picked up my phone, and I smiled for a picture. He held it up while I gave the toast.

"To the world we dream of," I said raising the "one" cupcake in my right hand, "and to the world we live in," I said raising the "zero" cupcake in my left. To the world I dream of for my company, and the world she is born in: 2020.

Bless that man for recording it on video.

* * *

Those two moments were significant, but not as great as New Year's Day. When Andrew left the next morning, I realized I still had two cupcakes in the fridge. Fuck yeah! I ran to the fridge and shoved them in my mouth. Like a boss. Ahem, like THE boss.

PART 2

LOUNGE LIFE

CHAPTER 7

IN THE BEGINNING...

———

The meeting of two personalities is like the contact of two chemical substances: if there is any reaction, both are transformed.

—CARL GUSTAV JUNG

January 2, 2020

My first business trip has arrived! It's really going to happen—Like really-really! I'm building out a Trello board for my schedule like I would if I was the best assistant ever.

This feeling reminds me of a rear detachment commander I knew back in my Army spouse days. When a unit deploys, especially a large one like a battalion or division, a group stays "in the rear" to hold things together while the fighting happens "forward." My first and only husband, so far, was in Iraq, and I had to drop off paperwork, or something, so I stopped by.

I walked in and the captain, a young blonde woman in uniform, was staring at the ceiling and leaning back in her office chair. She was slowly spinning around. I could hear her mumbling, "I don't want to be a commander. I want to be a princess."

She was having a worse day than I was. It's probably been fifteen years since, and this is one of the memories my brain decided to keep. Thanks, brain.

Well, I don't want to be planning this trip. I want to be a princess! This is exciting, but it would be better if I knew what the hell I was doing. I still have a couple days to set things up, but I'm spending big money on this trip, and I want to maximize it.

"Big money" is the term for any dollar that exits my account. I paid $274.01 for a roundtrip ticket from Austin to DCA. I can't imagine a cheaper fare—especially to DCA. It's always nice to avoid the big Dulles International Airport and crazy traffic on the dreaded beltway.

I'm slightly distracted by the view in front of me. I'm at my "desk" in the WeWork at Barton Springs, and it has a panoramic view of the Austin skyline. I came here in April 2019 for a Georgetown University alumni event and gushed about the view to everyone I met. It was evening, so the city was sparkly. I guess you get used to it because most folks responded to my enthusiasm by asking when I moved to Austin.

Speaking of WeWork, I should go grab another Americano. Every cup of coffee or espresso I drink is a double win: it is free now, and I can mentally deduct it from the cost of the enormous annual fee on DEFIANT's AmEx.

* * *

Cheers!

I settle back in to work with my Americano and the sparkly skyline. It looks like glitter in the Texas sun.

Hey glitter girl! Focus. I still have a couple areas where I could build in a meeting or a dinner.

A few months ago, back in October during the AUSA conference, a friend sent me an email introduction that went nowhere. It was from Danny, the chief data officer for Artifio, a cybersecurity company, to their vice president of business development (BD). What was her name? I search my emails and oh wow, I'd barely responded. Yikes.

Email: January 2, 2020 11:32 a.m.

Hi Heather,

I'm popping into D.C. next week. Any chance you're at the McLean office? I'd love to connect.

Best,

Julie

It was worth a shot. I kept working and eventually packed it up to go home. I stopped at a friend's house to check on their cats on the way home because that's what single people do during the holidays. I was on my iPad on their sofa when I saw Heather's response.

Email: January 2, 2020 5:09 p.m.

Hi Julie! Calling you in one hour. What is your mobile? Thanks, Heather

Oh shit! I wrote her back and hurried home to be ready for her call. She did not call me one hour after sending her email. She did not call one hour after my reply giving her my cell. She did call, though, and we talked for two hours.

"You've got to meet Nina."

"Oh great, do you think she has time next week?" I will maximize the $274.01 I spent on that flight if it's the last thing I do.

"Probably, but she's in San Diego."

What the… Okay, sure. I'm trying to figure out how to leverage my first trip, but yeah… why not go to San Diego next? It's only my life savings. My network is in D.C. and face-to-face communication is the way BD is done in the government. If I want to land my first client, an e-sports company looking to establish their brand credibility internationally, I need to brainstorm with Edward and connect some dots.

It would be great if I could come back from this trip and pitch to them an opportunity to host e-sports events in China and South Korea, since they have headquarters there, at an American diplomatic facility (embassy/consulate/etc.) or with diplomatic staff. The company is also headquartered in America, making the same opportunity possible with the Chinese and South Korean diplomatic facilities here.

"Okay great, tell me about Nina." Yeah, good idea. Find out who she is before you book the flight. I'm getting the hang of this.

"Nina joined us from Google. She'd be a great person to connect you with. She is our marketing director and the one with the budget."

Heather is talking and I'm looking at flights. Holy crap, there is one for $127—one way, from Vegas!

No, I haven't lost my mind. I'm trying to capitalize on a trip to see my Aunt Mary in St. George, Utah. She's on her third year of stage-four breast cancer, so the more I can see her the better. Plus, we have a lot in common. My sister is mini-Mom. I'm mini-Aunt Mary. My mom and stepdad winter down there, so I plan to catch up with everyone in a few weeks. Coincidentally, my friend Jessica is having her birthday party in Vegas that weekend. I can hop over to San Diego and fly back to Austin before February.

I buy the flight to San Diego to meet Nina. After the wild ride my darling ex has me going on next week to D.C., I'm starting to believe I have the best job ever!

* * *

Good morning, Washington! I've missed you. I love you. I'm hungry.

First stop: breakfast with the great and wonderful Kyle! I chose the same proper napkin place I went to at the conclusion of AUSA, because it's the closest thing to hotel breakfast a girl staying in her ex's spare bedroom is gonna find.

What happened next is *the* scene I will forever go to when I'm working out and the trainer says, "go to your happy place." Give me a minute to set this up.

I'm walking up Pennsylvania Avenue by the International Monetary Fund building. Big spacious sidewalk, no one really around, and lots of sunshine bouncing off the glass buildings all make it feel like spring in D.C. even though the weather report says there'll be snow later.

I see Kyle a block away crossing the street. Kyle sees me. The people behind Kyle look very confused. Very, very confused. Why? Because he starts running. It's the classic ending scene of a romantic comedy. We hug. We say hello. We are happy.

In his hand is an envelope with my name on it. A large office stationery envelope. He'd written me a letter.

What?

Yeah.

Do you get why I adore this man? He had no idea why I was in town, neither did I, but he didn't even realize I'd started DEFIANT. As soon as we had settled in at our table in the restaurant and ordered coffee, I told him.

He was ecstatic—ready to help, ready to support, ready to introduce me around, and whatever else it is wonderful people living in cults do to encourage others to join. The last time I saw Kyle was during the week between Christmas and New Years in 2018. The city was dead, but Kyle was in town. I met up with him at his office on K Street, which in D.C.-speak means he's doing well. It didn't take long before I realized he'd slept there the night before.

He took me to a conference room with delicious snacks and a suitcase in the corner. The dry-erase walls were covered with writing like the trees and rocks in *Cast Away*. Kyle explained he'd slept under the conference table, and at some point, he got up and stole the sofa cushions from the lobby furniture to lay on.

I was jealous. I wanted a life where my work was so important that I couldn't waste time commuting. Kyle was living my dream! Give me a sofa cushion and a quiet conference room—GAME ON.

Sometimes when I tell that story people think I'm a little nutty to be jealous. I've learned it's okay that some people don't understand. Not everyone wants their work to be the center of their world. Also, it's the difference between salary and hourly attitudes—mission driven vs punching a clock.

Kyle isn't just committed to his creation, but his creation is committed to improving the world we live in. To me, Kyle has everything. He has purpose and an unwavering heart to see it through.

Okay, enough doting on Kyle. For now.

* * *

AUSA agreed to meet with me between my proper napkin breakfast meeting and an early afternoon coffee meeting. Meetings and meetings and meetings, oh my!

Yes, this is the same AUSA from the big conference back in October and the one in 2018 that detonated the bomb in my chest. Amazing what a little trauma therapy can do, isn't it? Today I stayed at AUSA so long they fed me lunch. We talked all things AFC and the event they were hosting in June: FUTURES. My goal is to be their Austin consultant, not only because I needed to get paid, but also because it is a great fit.

AUSA and AFC want to connect academia, industry, entrepreneurs, and the Army. I speak three out of four of those languages, and as the daughter of a retired professor, I understand a little academia, too. AUSA seems keen on hiring me and a little overwhelmed. Perfect! I'm great at convincing people everything will be fine.

Except the weather turned, and it started angry snowing. I just had felt spring with Kyle a few hours ago, remember? My coffee meeting was three blocks away. I can totally do this! I blew into that cafe like Mary Poppins—if she didn't have an umbrella and was caught in a flippin' snowstorm.

I barely knew the woman I met there, Amanda. We'd met once in Austin, and I knew she was active in the military modernization ecosystem. It was a great conversation, even though it started out as business—D.C. business.

"What can I do for you?" she asked.

Oh honey, no.

"Nothing. Maybe something later, but I really just wanted to get to know you," I said. It's terrible how people in D.C. are conditioned to believe someone only wants to spend time with them to use them. At least D.C. is up front about it.

Austin, on the other hand, is less overt and more enthusiastic but just as transactional.

The conversation changed after that. We talk about boys, life, the bullshit of being a woman in this ecosystem, and the hysterical moments that keep us afloat. I tell her about a trip I was on with a two-star general, and that the guy conducting the classified briefing winked at me.

The general's aide, a captain, was sitting right next to me. He slowly turned his head in my direction and tried to give me the "did I just see what I think I saw" eyes. Sweet Cody. The guy did it again later, too. I didn't see Cody for almost a week and when we finally connected at the office, we blurted out what we'd wanted to say in that briefing.

"Do you know him?" he asked as I simultaneously said, "I've never met that man."

Poor sweet Cody. It didn't occur to him that random winking in the office was still a thing in 2019. Amanda and I laugh.

* * *

Now is a good time to explain why I have coffee and breakfast meetings. Happy hour implies drinking, drinking implies lowered inhibitions, and lowered inhibitions imply trouble. Ergo therefore… happy hour equals trouble.

The same logic applies to dinners. Business dinners are trouble. I don't like them. They're more appropriate than happy hours, but less appropriate than coffee or breakfast. Breakfast is business. It's time at the trough before a nine o'clock morning meeting. It's perfect because everyone has the opportunity to express their self-importance by stating they have a meeting they have to run to, or some other matter.

Breakfast is perfect. Coffee can be, too. But coffee can linger. One must be careful.

None of that logic applies to Catherine, though. I'd meet with her at 3:00 a.m. if that's what she had open. She probably doesn't, though. She is a fancy and powerful butt-kicker. Foreign actors have done terrible, terroristic things to her property in the United States. She's tougher than all of us.

I met her on a spin bike at the Alexandria YMCA in 2017. We were putting our spin shoes on, and I mentioned I was going to an event that night in D.C.

"Which one?" she asked, "I have an event tonight, too."

"Oh, some friends and I are going to the Kennedy Center," blah blah blah, I blabbered on. "You?"

"I got invited to the White House Correspondents Dinner, but I'm going to the wrong one."

"Wow! Wait, the wrong one?"

"Yeah. I'm going to the real one not the fun one Samantha B. is doing."

I've wanted to be Catherine ever since that moment. If I'm in town, I'm going to check to see if I can get a few minutes to soak in her badass presence. Back in 2018, she called me from an airport lounge in something-stan to ensure I was following her advice. I was going through a wicked learning experience as a contractor, and she made the time to be in my corner.

She is my breakfast date for the second day of this trip, and we meet at the last place we'd had post-spin class brunch. We talked until I got a text from a friend at the Pentagon saying he had to move our meeting. It was either now or not this trip.

UBER!

I spent the rest of the day at an off-site location—much easier than getting me through security. We expanded on the Pentagon's plan to get professional athletic training and conditioning for today's soldiers. It was brilliant, and all I did was integrate their plan and tie a pretty bow on it.

Then, I crashed back at Edward's place. I stopped at the Whole Foods hot bar and stuffed my face alone in his kitchen. He's never home. I've seen him come home at 4:00 a.m. and go back out at 6:00 a.m., only to return after 9:00 p.m. that night. Secretly I've wondered if he's powered by cocaine, but he's just like Kyle. His work matters—to him and to making it so you and I wake up today in our happy little bubbles.

* * *

When I chose my return flight to Austin, I made sure I could see my trauma therapist before I had to be at the airport. Even if I hadn't seen Kyle, Catherine, or AUSA, at least I would have seen her.

CHAPTER 8

VEGAS

——

Be open to things changing, it's going to be better than you planned.

—PAULO COELHO, THE ALCHEMIST

When I booked this trip, I chose a one-way flight to St. George, Utah because I didn't know if I wanted to swing through Vegas for Jessica's birthday. She celebrates there every year because it happens to overlap with ShotShow. ShotShow is *the* conference for gun runners. If you sell a handgun, or something similar, this is where you go to display your wares. It's the AUSA for weapons. Jessica prefers her men extra special—special forces special. So, every year she books a suite at the Venetian and enjoys the view. I'm not the Vegas kind. I don't drink. I like sleep. I'm dating Andrew. So, I plan to work and eat.

My sister and brother were invited. Not to ShotShow—oh my god, not to ShotShow. They were invited to St. George. It's just a drive, or shuttle ride, from Vegas. They didn't come. Was I ticked? Yes. Will I get over it? Eh, sure.

Once again, because this isn't my first trip to St. George since my Aunt Mary's third cancer diagnosis (yes, third), I shack up at the glamorous Comfort Inn. The towels are clean and somehow TBS is always playing *Big Bang Theory*. Breakfast comes with single-serve peanut butter cups. Can't get that at home.

We do the thing. We spend the time. We eat the food. I drive off with my mom and stepdad to spend a night in a yurt. Why? Because that's what you do when your parents have everything. Not in a Venetian suite kind of way, but in the "what would I do with that?" way. They need nothing.

"What are you getting your parents for Christmas?" Andrew asked one night back in December.

"We're staying in a yurt out in Zion National Park when I visit in a couple weeks," I said.

"So, nothing."

He's not wrong, but it was really funny at the time. The joke holds up. It's not much of anything, just quality time together and a shared experience that combines s'mores and scenery. It was gorgeous! Snow on the mountains and we made hot dogs. Quality family time, folks.

The next day we drove back to St. George, and they dropped me off at the Vegas shuttle stop. Yeah, I decided to go to ShotShow because it's work, right? I don't know yet. Onward to crazy town!

* * *

ShotShow is nuts. It is full batshit crazy nuts—classic Vegas. I landed at the airport, hopped in a cheap shuttle van, and grabbed an Uber to the hotel. Jessica said she left a key at the hotel desk for me, and they were already rolling out to a nearby hotel. Apparently, the *Military Times*, a well-read newspaper in the defense industry, was hosting a happy hour and we were on the list. Us? How? I have no idea.

I changed clothes and pumped up my makeup. There's no way I was going to get to Vegas level, but I wanted to lose the "I woke up in a yurt" look.

It has been years, if not a decade, since I picked up a *Military Times* paper. I'm not really the *Military Times* type. I didn't think they'd let me roll in off the casino floor, but it worked. Ha! I did the old "Yes, I am on the list. I'm the last one to arr... oh, there they are. Yes, thank you." Did I mention how crazy hot my friend Jessica is? Of course, we were on the list! What was I thinking?!

The bar itself wasn't great scenery, but I will tell you I met a man (wow, wow, wow, wow... not like that) I hope to stay connected with. Remember what I said about happy hours? Yep.

Enter Benjamin—gorgeous former Navy SEAL, model, and reality television show dude. Only in America.

Now that I'm a businesswoman, I only talk about business. I'm like a mommy scrolling through my phone to show strangers photos of my baby, while holding my baby.

"My startup is three weeks old now... so, things are going well." We laughed.

Benjamin had startup experience. He is now a partner at a company which makes tactical gear. He understood my hustle better than anyone else in the bar.

Eventually, I brought up my trip to San Diego. Nina, the woman Heather told me I had to meet, was proving too elusive for me. She was fully non-responsive. So, now that I was heading to San Diego to meet Nina and not actually getting to meet Nina, I needed a new plan—fast.

"Hey, you were a SEAL. You must know people in San Diego." Subtle start, Jules. "My dinner on Wednesday fell through. Do you know anyone I should meet?" Shh... he doesn't need to know I planned to eat a hotel marketplace lean cuisine. (Kidding, that's too many carbs)

Benjamin thinks about it for a second and asks me for my number. I gave it to him. Thirty seconds later, a group text pops up:

Text January 20, 2020 9:54 p.m.

Benjamin: Ryan, meet my friend Julie. She will be in SD this Wednesday. Please have dinner with her. I told her about your company, and she is interested in learning more. She works with applied sciences/strategic communications for the military. I am meeting with her about my company as well. Good person to know.

Me: Thank you, Benjamin! Ryan, I'm heading to San Diego, and I'd love to chat about what your company is doing and where you're headed.

Ryan: Perfect. Let's do it... In spite of you knowing Benjamin. Shoot me some options.

In addition to dinner with Ryan, I'd invented two other reasons to be in San Diego so the trip won't feel like a giant waste of money, if Nina never materializes. Both were connections at Artifio, the same company Danny and Heather work for: Matt, a former c-suite guy, and Brandon, a current BD guy I met in October at AUSA. I'm a little disappointed it didn't occur to me to reach out to Matt until halfway through the movie *1917*, but I'll forgive myself.

Don't worry, I'm going to explain why a World War I movie compelled me to reach out to a man I hadn't spoken to in months. I'll tell you more about Matt when I get to San Diego, but for now you only need to know one thing: Matt is an operational outsider in the intelligence community (IC). He knows people. He knows people who do things—things I want to do, things that impact lives, things I'd sleep under a conference room table for.

A week and a half ago, Andrew and I had a hot date on the books to see *1917*. I didn't care about the movie. I just wanted to sit in a dark theater and zone out while holding his hand. Doesn't that sound nice? I wish I was doing that right now and not in a casino bar with showy, shadowy men.

Somewhere in the middle of the movie, it hit me like a lightning bolt. Matt. Matt! MATT! I knew I needed to see Matt because I want DEFIANT to do the things that impact lives. Vague, yes. I managed to make it through the rest of the movie without grabbing my phone and texting him. I made it all the way to 8:23 a.m. the next morning.

Text January 12 8:23 a.m.

Me: Good morning! I'm popping over to San Diego on the 22nd and 23rd. I'd love to say hi if you're in town.

Fingers were tapping…

Text January 13, 11:58 a.m.

Matt: Hi. As of my current schedule I will be around. Let me know your schedule and where you'll be, and we can arrange some time. Happy New Year!

9:31 p.m.

Me: Your text made my day! I am free after 3:00 p.m. on the 22nd or before noon on the 23rd. I should be bouncing between Point Loma and Gaslamp. Happy to uber anywhere.

My desperation is transparent and genuine. It really did make my day. Now I have dinner with a guy who makes fabric and lunch with Matt. I also have a very loose coffee plan with Brandon. Brandon is Thor, a former green beret built quite literally like Thor. He's a nice guy. I reached out on LinkedIn hoping he could help me meet up with Nina. Fail, but he can have coffee with me.

Cool. I guess going to meet Nina was never about meeting Nina.

CHAPTER 9

FOLLOW THE MONEY

———

Forget what they told you. You want the truth, follow the money.

—ROXANNE BLAND

I survived the first night in Vegas. One night down, and one to go.

The hotel is gorgeous. The room is beautiful and spacious enough for four women and all their trappings. Yes, four women. Did I not mention this was a group thing? Yeah, I didn't know either. I knew I wasn't the only person invited, but I didn't know I'd be sleeping in a king bed with another woman.

The real question here is: did I know her name before I crawled in bed with her? Nope.

One quick follow up question: did she spoon me? Yep.

I laid very still like we were reenacting the Jeep scene from *Jurassic Park*. I played the part of the human by not moving until she, playing the part of the T-Rex, moved on. Not the weirdest thing to happen in that hotel room last night, but I'm trying to forget getting up to pee at 3:00 a.m. and walking in on two naked people in the bathroom. I guess that's the price of having a small bladder.

Once it was really morning, I showered, got dressed, and took my laptop with me to find somewhere to work. Hustlers gotta hustle. Make sure you pronounce the 'l' in there for me. Otherwise I sound like a hussy.

I found a six dollar cup of coffee and a little bistro table to pretend to work on. I need to review the proposal I sent to AUSA before our call in an hour. I also need a lot more caffeine. Let me clarify, cheaper caffeine.

* * *

For anyone watching the clock, and I know I am, I've been reviewing the proposal with AUSA for two full hours. Halfway through I told them I needed to head upstairs to my hotel. We broke for fifteen minutes, long enough for me to pop into the chocolate shop (I know, right?) and get to the room.

I know a lot about what they are trying to do, but I am clueless about their operations. It's a nonprofit, so of course I've poured through their financial records—990 forms are my jam. They may not tell me where every dollar comes from or where it goes, but they always tell me how the money moves.

AUSA is a multi-million-dollar machine—upwards of thirty million dollars a year.[2] Some years, they make upwards of forty-seven million dollars.[3]

Money flows in from memberships and sponsorships. Back in my Army spouse days, we were members. My ex-husband probably still is because you can't leave the mafia. It's like if your college alumnae association had power over your career. You'd probably give them forty dollars a month, too.

Our forty dollars was hardly worth their effort to collect. I didn't know it at the time, but the millions and millions in their operating budget come from the hundreds and hundreds of thousands of big company sponsorships. Industry, a.k.a. the big boys that make up the defense contractors, kindly sponsor events throughout the year. Sometimes they even pay to attend these events. For example, a six-figure sponsorship at the annual meeting in October will buy you a nice booth near the front door. It may even buy you plush carpet for your cannon to sit on. It depends on the first number of those six figures.

Keep in mind, everyone knows cannons are notoriously glam and look best on plush carpet. You can't cheap out on cannon carpet.

AUSA's event in June—FUTURES—is not ready for sponsorship, yet. They will be. Right now, they're trying to navigate Austin and the back and forth they're getting locally.

2   Internal Revenue Service, (2017), Form 990: Return of Organization Exempt from Income Tax: Association of the United States Army Inc. Retrieved from the ProPublica database.

3   Internal Revenue Service, (2016), Form 990: Return of Organization Exempt from Income Tax: Association of the United States Army Inc. Retrieved from the ProPublica database.

Support from the top is assured. I was there. General Ham, the retired four-star general currently holding court as the President of AUSA, looked me in the eye back when I worked for AFC and asked if I could deliver an e-sports tournament in June.

"Yes, sir."

The five other big wigs from AFC at General Murray's conference table watched in horror as I committed us to delivering on something they'd probably never seen. But I knew I could pull this one off. My friend in Austin owned a company focused on doing just this. Check!

Two hours of guiding AUSA through any potential ecosystem ego conflicts and away from trouble spots gave me more than enough time to eat the chocolate I bought. Damn it. At the end of the conversation, we'd agreed I was to deliver a new proposal with a flat rate (20 percent lower than my first one) for their leadership to sign.

So many shiny stars up there at AUSA. It's like the Milky Way sometimes.

Okay, fine. I'll do it for less. But now I have to figure out how to leverage the hell out of this opportunity. Sounds like a great task for all my down time in San Diego!

Shaking my fist to the sky... damn you Nina!

CHAPTER 10

ALL ROADS LEAD TO MATT

———

All the world's a stage, and all the men and women merely players....

—WILLIAM SHAKESPEARE

I guess I don't warrant Nina's love. I tried. I emailed, I LinkedIn messaged, and I had others in her company reach out. She does not want to bother with me.

Cool. It's 1:00 p.m. in San Diego, and I'm sitting on my bum in my hotel room. Oh boy.

Brandon and I are meeting in an hour and a half at a cute little coffee shop nearby. I chose this hotel because a) it's the least expensive Marriott property near b) where Nina and Brandon work. It's new. It's nice. I'm in the middle of doing hotel laundry in an actual washer, not washing clothes in the bathroom sink.

It's pretty classy, therefore I'm pretty classy by default.

The coffee shop is a twenty-five-minute walk from me, and it looks adorable online. I'll head out the door as soon as my clothes come out of the washer. I really hope they're not destroyed. My experience with hotel laundry is limited to when I moved to Austin and lived in hotels for thirty days. It was during SXSW last year (2019). I was told my job was moving to Austin, and if I wanted to come with it, I'd get a little cash for the move and thirty days of meals and hotels. I could also rent a car. Woohoo!

Since I had two weeks to figure out the move and show up, my hotel choices were limited. Uncle Sam is not a "market rate" kind of guy, so I ended up staying progressively further and further away from town during that month. By the end, after working fourteen SXSW events in four days, in one capacity or another, I was grateful my final stay was in beautiful Texas Hill Country. My timesheet for that pay period maxed out Monday (eighty hours in two weeks), so after spending Tuesday in bed eating peanut butter and watching *Game of Thrones* I putzed around the trails the rest of the week.

When I was in San Diego back in October with Ann, I realized this was the time in my life to start a business. It's not hard to feel inspired when surrounded by eighty-two-degree sunshine. One of many fabulous things about San Diego is the weather, and the same sun greets me as I pop out to work at Moniker. Google and Yelp thought I'd like it, so why not?

I could live here. The people are friendly, and the weather is delightful. It's intimidatingly fit, but I'm used to that in Austin. Oh my god, the abs in Austin. If you ever visit, go down to the trail and watch them go by. Incredible.

Oh, this is adorable. Sometimes I wonder why I'm friends with humans; Google and Yelp know me so much better than people. It's big and bright and bustling. Happy folks are working and chatting. It smells like the sweet nectar of the gods: coffee. The space feels vintage but updated. It's perfection!

I explain my exuberance to the poor guy behind the counter, Conor, and he's polite about it. He is a big fan of Austin, so we get along well. He invites me to take a table and wait for my Americano. Don't mind if I do, Conor.

Brandon walks in early, as you'd expect. He's enormous—not out of proportion in his own skin, but out of proportion with other mortals. He fits the expansive space well. The man must be six-and-a-half feet tall, broad—presumably ripped—shoulders, and he's wearing a vest. Fuck, me. I'm a sucker for vests—vests in three-piece suits, vests with jeans.

There's a double yellow line with vests. Fleece vests are not okay. Leather vests are not okay. Brandon is doing a service to the vest, and the vest is certainly doing a service for Brandon.

I consider telling him that, but I don't really know this man. And yeah, I probably have ten years on him. He's adorable. We met at AUSA in October by accident. I was getting permission at booths for the ridiculously talented Travis to shoot video when General Murray was scheduled to make his rounds later that day. It's always nice to let folks know you'll be coming by with a camera. The first thing most people do is run their tongue over their teeth, but whatever works.

I didn't see Brandon, despite his presence. He was standing next to a woman with purple curly hair and I freaked.

"EMILY!"

She turns and greets me with a big hug. I'd just derailed whatever conversation they were having. But there was another woman in here, a "younger" woman (relatively speaking), and it was Emily! I don't know how I met Emily, but she is a trailblazer in the national security world. She started a community, a conference, and a speaker series for women in national security. It's the only space for the interns and beyond to belong.

She and I had coffee a couple times when I started at AFC. We were just acquaintances... until she admitted to not liking the organization my ex, Hal, worked for. From that moment on, we've been friends.

Going into this coffee shop with Brandon, the only context he had of me was that I'd crashed his conversation with Emily at AUSA. He was a trouper. All I knew about Brandon was he worked at Artifio and was prior something. I didn't know he was a green beret, but that fits.

We talked everything: politics, defense, and entrepreneurship. It was lovely. He's a good dude and sharper than I gave him credit for. I knew he'd be a bit salesy because he's in business development, but I didn't know he'd be generally smart. It's not because I don't think Thor has a brain, it's because I don't always meet the brightest bulbs. I'm just being honest here.

I left our extra-long conversation with two takeaways. First, it's possible to get a "finder's fee" and a "success fee" from the capture management companies. WHAT? Second, Matt's wife was the recruiter who brought Brandon to the organization. All roads somehow lead to Matt.

I pounced on the idea of getting paid to send tech companies to the capture folks. It makes total sense, but I didn't know it was a thing. I knew capture management existed, but I didn't realize they needed folks like me to send companies their way. The small businesses win by getting SBIR money and the warfighter wins by getting disruptive tech.

Here's how it works. I suggest taking a break, stretching your legs, and grabbing a cup of coffee before reading further.

* * *

I'm going to refer to DEFIANT in the plural because, as my grandma always said, "hope springs eternal." I'm lumping the terms "acquisitions" in with "procurement" for the purpose of this being a primer. However, think of acquisitions as Broadway and procurement as the theaters.

Procurement is a system of processes protected from corruption by layers of bureaucracy. This process is neither effective nor efficient, but it is the process we have. If you remember back when I left AFC, I was helping the military communicate with the innovation community. Along the way, with the bumps and bruises to prove it, I realized I would be more effective if I turned the equation around. DEFIANT's mission is to help startups, small businesses, researchers, etc. communicate their capabilities to the military. To do that, we've advised potential clients that there are two paths to get a contract with the military. The first is the traditional path of solving a problem the bureaucracy has identified (called "requirements"), and the second is a myriad of new processes developed and modified over the last few years.

There is overlap between the two paths, so therefore, we treat the ecosystem as a whole. This principle—holistic procurement—shapes how we approach communicating to the procurement ecosystem. We begin by categorizing the target audience into layers and players.

Layers are the paperwork checkpoints and the regulatory flaming hoops to jump through. Players are the people who create, abide by, or disrupt those checkpoints and hoops. Layers don't have opinions or feelings about the process. People (a.k.a. players) do. However, both can be influenced and must be communicated with separately and strategically.

"Influence" is a four-letter word in the minds of the military and government. Neither the defense nor the intelligence community shall influence American citizens. Whenever I used this word in the four walls of AFC, I'd preface it with "I don't know what other word to use here..." and sometimes I'd say "targeting" just to watch their heads explode. Targeting is a sport, an art, and a science. It's what they do to terrorists, so the mention of "targeting" in a downtown skyscraper is a strategic way to buy yourself time. (You lose them for a minute.) Seriously, if you need to take a sip of water or check your notes, work it into a sentence.

Let's identify the layers and players:

LAYERS

- Federal Acquisition Register (FAR)

- Federal Business Opportunities (FedBizOpps or FBO)

- Data Universal Numbering System (DUNS)

- System for Award Management (SAM)

- Doctrine (National Defense Strategy, National Security Strategy, Multi-Domain Operations, etc.)

- Budget (NDAA, etc.)

RESOURCES:
- General Services Administration (GSA)

- Minority Business Development Agency (MBDA)

- Procurement Technical Assistance Program (PTAP)

- Small Business Administration (SBA)

RESEARCH AND DEVELOPMENT (R&D) PROCUREMENT:

"Part thirty-five of the FAR provides guidance on R&D contracting. Interested companies, organizations, and other entities may use FedBizOpps to identify R&D opportunities, which may be posted as solicitations or broad agency announcements (BAA)."[4]

That's the first path—the open solicitation method where the government posts what they need and industry bids on answering that need with a solution. The second path, often termed "nontraditional," has gained popularity in recent years.

Nontraditional procurement methods for R&D, include unsolicited proposals (Subpart 15.6 of the FAR) and challenges. These are the fun ones that allow for creativity to seep into our bureaucracy. Instead of asking industry to solve a problem the government has defined, the government asks industry to identify a problem and provide the solution. Often this solution needs R&D money.

Organizations have sprung up in the ecosystem to include Defense Innovation Unit (DIU, formerly DIUx), AFWERX, NavyX (now NavalX), National Security Innovation Network (NSIN, formerly MD5), Army Futures Command, and Army

---

4   "Overview of the Federal Procurement Process and Resources," Every-CRSReport, January 16, 2015.

Venture Capital Initiative. By the time this book is published, it's likely one of those names no longer exists or has merged with another one. Whatever they call themselves, the modernization movement is carved in doctrine (National Defense Strategy), blessed by Congress, monitored by the Office of Management and Budget, and is ultimately responsible for linking Silicon Valley terminology with the Pentagon.

An unfortunate side effect, and one to be avoided at all costs, is association with the "innovation theater" phenomenon. "Innovation theater" is any engagement that appears to be connected to modernization but is insincere. If a check can't be cashed at the end of the event, it's theater. For example, when people say the Army is modernizing and then someone asks for data to back that up—awkward.

PLAYERS

I preface this section with an unusual saying from the executive leadership coach I had during graduate school: organizations are faithless whores. When it comes to bureaucracy, remember they are not loyal to the people who serve them, and those individuals carry career-ending risk if they violate their organization's norms. It is possible, however, to navigate this and protect players.

The dark side of bureaucracy aside, rising stars and influencers exist in the procurement ecosystem. Some players lead movements of change and some lay low, neither agreeing with criticism of the Layers nor refuting it. Those players are usually in the category of fearing the consequences of violating norms. Some defend the status quo. It's a mixed audience, and a few players have published papers out of their studies at the National War College on the subject of modernization.

My favorite Major General (MG), if I'm allowed to pick favorites here, is MG Patrick Burden. He has the best smile and is just the nicest human being. Back when COL Patrick Burden's War College thesis on modernizing the acquisition process was published, the year was 2010. Today, MG Patrick Burden is the king of Combat Systems (oops, typo: director). Reading his paper, "Acquisition Reform - What's Really Broken in Defense Acquisition," hurts. He very clearly lays out the case for change in the abstract with, "If we do nothing to address the need to get capabilities to our military forces in a more timely manner, we will continue to lose critical resources (personnel, funding, and time) allocated for the defense of our country, which will also limit our technological advantage around the world." [5]

Is it any wonder why he's my fave? As much as I appreciate his paper, it frustrates me that we're ten years in the future with the same problem set. He had the ideas ten years ago and has the title now. If he can't make changes, who can? Also, I think if you read his thesis, you'll wish his recommendations had been implemented, too.

INTERNAL PLAYERS
Individual players include the MG Patrick Burdens of the world but also vary from a new recruit to a legislator—venture capitalists to career civilians. All the chatty Cathys on social media fall into this category.

---

5   Colonel Patrick W. Burden, "Acquisition Reform—What's Really Broken in Defense Acquisition," (Senior Service College Fellowship Civilian Research Project, U.S. Army War College, 2010), 1-42.

Media has a huge influence on the system. The individual reporters certainly do, too. Another external influencer is the think tank community. An interesting trend is the use of think tanks in the United Kingdom to shop ideas. When a policy maker or general wants to test a new idea/process/product/capability, they do it overseas first. Don't believe me? Look into how the former U.S. Army Europe Commander Lt. Gen. Ben Hodges used the media through think tanks to communicate to Congress.

Absolutely brilliant, if you're into that kind of thing. "Make 30,000 soldiers look like 300,000," was his catch-phrase. [6] Think about that. You can find him holding court as the Pershing Chair in Strategic Studies at the Center for European Policy Analysis (think tank), as a partner at Berlin Global Advisors (geopolitics and government affairs firm), and as Distinguished Fellow at the Royal United Services Institute for Defence and Security Studies (think tank). [7,8]

Chatham House rules for real.

There is also a sub-group of players known as the "O-6 Rolodex." O-6's in the Army are full bird Colonels, and as they approach retirement, they're often recruited by big defense companies to work for them. Some are hired for their leadership skills or extensive knowledge about a business line

---

6   John Vandiver, "How US Army Europe's outgoing general got the Pentagon's attention," STARS AND STRIPES, October 17, 2017.

7   "Lieutenant General (Ret'd) Ben Hodges," Royal United Services Institute (RUSI), accessed August 31, 2020.

8   "Geopolitics and Government Affairs," Berlin Global Advisors, accessed September 1, 2020.

(like tanks or planes), but their most valuable commodity is their Rolodex.

There is technically nothing wrong with hiring someone who plays well with others. In this context, the O-6 Rolodex is a network with hundreds of millions, if not billions, of dollars somewhere between the pages. We have a system that incentivizes retired officers to sell access to their buddies, and this is why we should all learn how to play golf. This girl is not a member of the retired O-6 Rolodex club. So, when potential clients ask who they need to talk to in order to get their disruptive technology into the hands of our warfighters, I don't have an answer.

You have to ask the O-6 Rolodex Mafia.

* * *

I leave Moniker and grab an Uber. I have no idea what traffic is like in San Diego, but I'm not going to be late for the dinner Benjamin set up for me at the *Military Times* happy hour in Vegas. It turns out, traffic isn't really a thing here. What a delightful, sunny place!

In the backseat I find myself looking for something near the restaurant to do while I wait for dinner. I'm always delighted when things work out, like they are right now. I see a highly rated nail salon in walking distance. San Diego, you spoil me.

All this and a bathroom, too!

* * *

Five hours later, I'm convinced the universe loves me. Ryan started a textile company that has sensors embedded in the fabric. Brilliant.

I think it would be great if he could get those on the bodies of soldiers. I suggested he look at SBIR funding. I don't know how that works, exactly, but I want to explore it.

CHAPTER 11

MERLIN

——

If the path be beautiful, let us not ask where it leads.
—ANATOLE FRANCE

Waking up in San Diego is nice. It's sunny, and I know if I just put on enough clothing to meet society's minimum for hotel breakfast buffets, everything will be amazeballs.

I love hotel breakfast, and I've had some stellar experiences. The food and atmosphere in the Singapore St. Regis comes to mind. If that's ten on a scale of one to ten, a regular Marriott buffet comes in at a solid six. For most folks there's more space between a luxury hotel and a Courtyard, but I'm not most folks. I'll let you in on a little secret: I'm in it for the small peanut butter cups and the Splenda. That's a six. If I could eat just peanut butter with Splenda, I would. Coffee and protein (eggs and sausage) take it to a seven. The bar is not high, I know that.

I go through the breakfast area and sit down to eat two peanut butter cups in plain view of our judgmental society, along with my eggs and sausage. Then, I grab four more cups and a handful of Splenda for the room before nonchalantly tossing a napkin on top to hide the gluttony. I feel like I've just stolen the queen's jewels. Not to be gross, but the mystery oil on top of the cheap peanut butter absorbs the Splenda and makes a crunchy crust. It's fucking delicious.

Back in the room, I complete my gluttony and prepare for a call with Justin, the guy who pays Brandon to act as a tech scout. Am I thinking the entire time about how I wish I had more peanut butter? Yes, yes I am.

Justin calls, and the conversation is momentous. Yes, it's possible to get paid to refer folks like the guy I had dinner with last night who makes the cool sensor fabric. Holy hell, Batman. Now we're in business! This is the kind of money that could sustain DEFIANT while I find my actual clients. Everyone wins—the companies, the warfighter, and DEFIANT.

Justin says he'll send me an associate referral agreement, and I jump off the call and right into an Uber. Off to lunch with Matt!

* * *

Matt has not aged. He lives in a California bubble of eternal health. I'm full of a corn syrup and corn oil crust sprinkled with my favorite chemical concoction (a.k.a. Splenda). I spent the ride up trying to remember how I met Matt. My first recollection is not about Matt, but about a little hottie body. I can't remember his name. I remember a lot about his thighs, and if I think about it too long, I'll never finish this story.

I had just come back from two weeks in Southeast Asia. The first week I was sampling the breakfast buffet at the St. Regis hotel in Singapore with my graduate school cohort from Georgetown University. The second week I was in a villa in Bali with fireflies lighting up the rice paddies that seemed to stretch on all night. Ubud is a special place if you can look past how the nouveau riche, boho chic, and yoga-vibing expats live surrounded by extreme poverty.

The week before, I was playing the part of one of those rich kids with my own butler to draw baths and bring me cappuccinos in the middle of the night at the six-star St. Regis. Six! Apparently, it's a thing. I was as far away as I could be from the contract I was on, and I was grateful for the distraction.

The day I left D.C. for Singapore, I'd cried—cried actual tears—to my boss about the toxic climate I was in on the client site. The crying spontaneously erupted in the St. Regis, too, and bonus, it was in front of my entire cohort. I was beyond unhappy on that contract and no longer able to put myself in that situation anymore. After bursting into tears in class, my friend Rebecca took me outside the classroom. She held both of my shoulders and demanded to know what was wrong. Behind her was a whole snack table with precious goodies and behind me was a man tending an espresso machine.

This is my vision of heaven. So, how is that the backdrop when my work situation broke me thousands of miles away?

The only thing I could come up with to say to her was, "I'm not going back there." "There" was not our hotel meeting room for the week, it was the office I worked in. That place was a federal cockfight. You see, government civilian employees can't be wrong. Their careers depend on being able to take the credit and deflect the blame. It's just part of the culture. So, who takes the blame? Contractors. Every day was another battle, and regardless of who was at fault, we lost.

Rebecca and I talked while she wiped my tears. Finally, after we stepped outside so she could smoke a cigarette, we regrouped and went back to join the cohort. I made an appointment to talk to my boss at 9:00 a.m. on the Monday of my return to D.C. It didn't matter what came out of it, just as long as I never went back to that office.

Corporate let me work from HQ, until they didn't, but that's a story for another book. The corporate office felt like heaven. The fridge didn't smell, and the coffee shop in the lobby brewed illycaffè.

On my second day working there, they gave me a hotel desk (that's when you work somewhere temporarily, but you don't bring a photo of your kids) and booked it for two weeks. It was fine by me.

Sasha, the front desk person and kindest heart in the building, showed me to my new desk. I'd clocked that little hottie body the moment we rounded the corner. She took me right next to his desk and told me to set up. She introduced me. Every day was leg day on his calendar—amazing.

He was also on the "bench," which is a contractor/consulting term for what you do when you're between billable contracts. Basically, he was looking for his next gig. It was either going to be with this company or somewhere else. This is the game contractors have to play. Yes, we are typically paid more, but we take the risk of a contract ending and being out of work. Don't get comfortable on the bench. Over the next few days, the little hottie body and I flirted, ahem, chatted enough that I passed his test, and he offered to send some introduction emails out to his network. Sweet little hottie body.

One of those emails went to Matt. It's funny how these windy roads take us to the strangest places. It started with a professional government cockfighting ring and a young man with a lunge addiction, and two years later I'm in an Uber in San Diego.

* * *

Funny story about that. After Matt and I met in 2018, he showed me inside the company he was working for, in the c-suite, and asked me to come up with a plan and pitch it to him. By the time that pitch day rolled around, I was his second meeting in the restaurant of the Westin in Alexandria, Virginia. He'd just finished breakfast, and I was sad I missed it. I'm a broken record, but it's my most favorite thing in the whole wide world.

I arrived early and took a table without seeing him. I ordered a small French press and pulled out my laptop to review my little pitch. Eventually, Matt came over and asked me to join him and his breakfast companion.

Matt taught me A LOT about life as a consultant. It's an obstacle course, and the whole thing is always changing. About a year later I learned that the man he was having breakfast with, who stuck around and heard my pitch, ran a detainment center overseas and oversaw policies we now consider extreme torture—not grade "A" torture, but the gnarly stuff that Hollywood won't even try to recreate.

And there I was with my little laptop and coffee—heels on, looking so cute, innocent, and idealistic. I wish I could bubble wrap that version of me and protect her from the real world. It's nice to remember myself that way.

* * *

"Matt!" I say, and we embrace. So nice to see him. When I think of Matt, I can't help but think how different my world would be if he'd just said yes to my proposal a few years ago. We don't talk about why it didn't work out and why he took me all the way to the edge. Somehow, it's not between us, though. I haven't seen him since the Westin a year and a half ago.

We talk about where our lives are. He's happy for me that I'm off doing DEFIANT. As you know, we're only here because I was hit by a bolt of lightning during *1917* a week and a half ago.

"I have to tell you why I had to reach out."

"Yes, please do."

I catch him up on Danny connecting me to Heather and my hunt for Nina. "I was just texting her," he gestures to his phone.

My face must have given away my immediate thought: excuse me, what?

"Yeah, I met Nina when we were considering bringing her in."

My inner voice, now politely muffled, is saying "fuck Nina, okay." My outside voice said, "Oh yeah that makes sense." The salmon salad is nice, but I could really go for a jar of peanut butter or a cake right now.

"So, you met with her?"

"Nope." I don't hide my disappointment, but I don't linger either. Nina was the reason for the plane ticket and taking a leap of faith, but my intuition led me to Matt. I tell him the story of watching *1917* in the theater and realizing I should reach out. "I remember we talked about, not the Africa project I was gunning for, but the one your friends were doing. I want to do that."

"Which one?"

"The ones who were enabling mission success."

It's vague, folks. We're in a restaurant, in a giant three-quarter-circle booth outside with other tables. He knew what I meant. You don't. That's how this part of the story ends for you.

For me, though, it is everything. It's why I'm there. I want Matt to know my heart is exactly where it was the last time we talked. He gets it.

"Oh Julie, if that's what you want check this out." He shows me a photo. The image on his phone reminds me of warships from *Star Trek*. My eyes bounce from the photo to his eyes, to the photo, to his eyes…

"It's real," he says. If this was the scene from a movie, I'd be the golden retriever with her head suddenly cocked to one side staring wide eyed at the human.

"I don't understand."

"Yeah."

Text January 23, 2020 1:14 p.m.

Matt: Vincent meet a friend and colleague of mine, Julie Willis. Julie meet Vincent who I spoke so highly of at today's lunch. Julie is a super sharp, world class connector, and change agent for companies in and out of military innovation. Please introduce yourselves here and segment time to have an introductory call. You will both be well served! Cheers, Matt

Vincent: Julie, it is a pleasure to meet you electronically via Matt's kind introduction. Have you ever seen Star Trek? I am building a weapons program designed to integrate soldiers. When successful it will be a game changer for every aspect of warfighter survivability.

Matt: Love it! Thanks for jumping right in. Keep me on your thread. You two can crush it together!!

Julie: Vincent, I have no idea what you're talking about, and I'm a little scared! I just left Army Futures Command as a contractor, and I don't think anyone asked if I'd seen Star Trek. There were plenty of baby Yoda Star Wars jokes, but not Star Trek. Anyway... Next Generation, yes.

"Where is this guy located?" I looked up from my phone and asked Matt.

"Reno."

"When are we going to Reno?"

The texts go on and on all afternoon. Between messages, I find a little sushi restaurant for dinner near my hotel. It was incredible and total happiness. I call Andrew and tell him all about my day. Part of the fun of my new world was sharing it with him because it was as foreign as life on Mars to an O-5 (lieutenant colonel) in the Army. His world operated like a spreadsheet, and mine looked like an abstract painting. All of it was weird to him—from flying somewhere without firm plans, to meeting someone I didn't know existed two days earlier, to the story about Merlin...

Why do I call him Merlin, and Matt calls him Vincent? Text 6:03 p.m.

Me: I do strategic communication (the knife edge of PR) when appropriate, but I'm a connector always. I was with AFC for over a year and never saw anything like your Lynx. You made magic, Vincent. You're a wizard. You're in my phone now as Merlin.

Merlin: "Merlin" that is probably the nicest call sign I have ever received, and what is your call sign ma'am?

I was given a new call sign when I moved to Austin. I arrived here a week or two after my friend Randy. Both of us were looking for apartments downtown, but Randy was not feeling the tall building experience. His call sign was Downtown Randy Clark. Mine became High Rise when I decided to live in a gleaming tower downtown. Out of context it could be taken... out of context.

* * *

I walk back to the hotel and turn on *Big Bang Theory*. How is it always on? I love Marriott hotels. I know they don't set television programming, but I don't have network television at home. So, to me, *Big Bang Theory* equals Marriott. However, Marriott does not equal *Big Bang Theory*, unless it is multiplied by peanut butter and Splenda.

I have an early morning flight tomorrow. I arrange a call with Merlin during my layover in LAX. I'm really getting the hang of this jet-setter entrepreneur life.

CHAPTER 12

THE MERLIN KING

———

she wasn't waiting for a knight

she was waiting for a sword.

—ATTICUS

I'm awake! I've gotta move or I'll miss the breakfast buffet before my flight, which is ironic because I want to get to the airport early enough to eat breakfast at the lounge.

I just need to check my flight details, and I see I have an email from Justin! This day is off to a good start.

Nope, not a good start at all. I read it again and again. I'm missing something. I start from the top.

My depression-era grandmother gave better gift cards than what Justin's offering in this agreement. In exchange for sending tech companies to them to do the proposal work, Justin is offering me 10 percent of their revenue minus their expenses.

Oh fun: fine print!

The 10 percent of their 10 percent is limited to Phase 1 and nothing if they pursue a Phase 2 (up to $750K) or are awarded a multi-million-dollar contract. According to this math, I'm cut out of the real money and I have no visibility into their expenses. Phase 1 is capped at what, $50K?

50,000/10=5,000 (their take of the R&D money)

5,000-"expenses"=?

?/10=less than $500

No. I know what Brandon is getting—a monthly retainer plus commission—and I'm worth as much. I'm out here hustling to find these companies and shepherd them through a process I only learned about two days ago. I realize the air is thin up here on my high horse, but thin air is better than hot air.

I shower. I steal peanut butter and Splenda. I grab coffee. I pack.

These guys, and I'm lumping Justin in with all the other alpha males I know, will try to get away with anything and everything. I could have sat down, typed out a nice reply, and countered his offer. I could have declined.

Instead, I wrote him back and walked out of the hotel.

"Justin, thank you for the email. Send me the real one."

* * *

I know you're on the edge of your seat here, and the answer is no. No, the hot buffet was not open that early at the hotel. The lounge is—thank the heavens. I need some proper napkin love.

I refuse to check my email. I am too angry and self-righteous. How dare he try to low ball me like that? Does he think I don't know math? Getting 10 percent of 10 percent of someone else's profit is nothing.

As I walk down the aisle to my seat, I realize something special. This is going in the book. Therefore, I guess I'm writing this thing. We can all blame Kyle for that. He called me last week as I was sitting at my Aunt Mary's dining room table with hair dye on my roots. In his velvety British accent, he told me it would be a great way to entice government officials and venture capitalists to meet for background interviews. He also said it would be criminal to not write this story.

I'm starting to understand why.

* * *

Hello LAX!

I've only been here once, and I accidentally left the airport and got on the bus to Disney. I was supposed to go to the next terminal. If this wasn't the cheapest Delta route back to Austin, I wouldn't be here.

It's ugly and angry in here. People look unhappy. I need to quickly—very quickly—find the Delta Lounge. Oh shoot, there are two—a North and a South. Which one is near my gate? I think the North one? Wait. They seem to be co-located. This is confusing and not nice to do to sleepy people.

Whatever. I'm up. I'm in. There is one seat available, and it is mine. "Mine, mine, mine," say the seagulls from *Finding Nemo* in my head.

My call with Merlin starts in five minutes. Okay, I need to pee and eat first.

* * *

Forty-five minutes pass and all I've managed to say is, "okay" over and over. I'd like to think I asked questions during this conversation, but I doubt it. Also, the filter in my brain clogged and stopped allowing information to pass through pretty early on. Why? Because our new friend Merlin is more than a wizard. He is king. I even said so out loud, which sounded as strange to the man across from me reading a newspaper as it did in my own head.

"Wait, you're king."

Merlin stopped his train of thought to ask, "What?"

"You're king. What you just described in addition to the *Star Trek* warship thing—the data, the way you capture it, the processing and analyzing, the things you can see and do— they make you king." He demurred like a classic nobleman.

Classic noblemen are my specialty. I've spent the majority of my adult life working with the warrior and noble classes. Goodness, I think just about every man I've ever dated was some form of a knight. They're protectors. They should form a reality show where they can be superheroes all day. Perhaps they already have a secret lair and meet for an annual conference in the hills of Colombia. Is this a James Bond plot? Focus, Jules.

Merlin brings me back with talk of things that go boom. I need another Americano. The conversation wraps up because I have to go find my gate. It occurs to me how strange I must look to the rest of the room. I'm not unfamiliar with the business of death and destruction, but this is next level. I couldn't shake the look on my face because I couldn't process the thoughts that made it take that shape.

Best to record this moment, I think. I take two seconds to do something I've never done before: snap a selfie of my face exactly the way it is. No angling to balance dark circles and double chins. The result was a woman who looks horrified but kind of hopeful for humanity. Well, she's horrified and hopeful. I'm adding humanity because, after all, aren't we who he's doing this for?

Quickly, I need to get to the gate. They are just starting to board. I call a computer-savvy friend with higher security clearance and lots of experience.

"Back in Austin?" she answers. I love how she starts conversations where she wants them.

"Not yet. I'm standing at the gate at LAX."

"I'm sorry. LAX is the worst."

She gets me.

"I need help."

"What kind of help?"

"I was just read in on a Deep Space Nine Borg project thing and I don't know what to do with the stuff on my computer. The guy sent me stuff, like photos and specifications and capabilities. I took notes. Now I'm afraid of my computer."

"Why are you afraid of your computer? Is any of it classified?"

"It should be!" I exclaim a little too loud for a crowded gate. "I don't know how it isn't. Do people out in the wild just do this? I mean, this is sensitive shit, and it's just on my dumbass laptop."

"Okay. Do you need help with file management?"

"That sounds like a thing I need. Yes."

"Okay."

"Okay? I mean, I used to have a laptop that Uncle Sam gave me, and he maintained all the things that keep it from giving away all the stupid PowerPoint quad charts saved on it. I don't know how to do that."

"Do what? Encrypt it?"

"Assume I don't know how to do anything."

"Okay. By the time you land I'll have something for you. I'll walk you through the entire thing, or we can get coffee this weekend and do it together."

"Oh my god, yes. Yes, please. I choose the coffee plan."

"Okay."

Her "okay" is way more assuring than the "okay" I gave Merlin.

PART 3

UH OH

CHAPTER 13

AUSA COMES TO AUSTIN

———

life is about the choices we make

the moments we don't see coming

and the strength to do

what's best for ourselves.
      —SAMANTHA KING, "BORN TO LOVE, CURSED TO FEEL"

Tralalalala lalalalalala

That's the sound joy makes in my head. I'm in CVS picking up goodies for the contingent from AUSA. They arrive tonight for a planning visit, and I want to leave little baggies of snacks at the hotel. I pick up two kinds of chocolates, a water bottle, a little note card, and a bag for each of the four people. Awesome possum.

Why didn't Google tell me how far away this hotel is? Holy mackerel, I'm sweaty. This is disgusting. It's a good thing I won't bump into them right now!

The folks at the front desk don't mind that I need to put my little presents together. They think I'm being cute. I think as soon as they turn their backs, I'm going to raid the breakfast buffet area and find the peanut butter. There are three of them. This is not going to be easy. Maybe I should just buy peanut butter.

I hand over my little bundles of joy to the front desk and leave, instead of creating a diversion and stealing peanut butter. It's for the best. I'll be back first thing in the morning for breakfast with the AUSA team.

Yeah, I scheduled that. When I say hotel breakfast is my favorite thing in the whole wide world, I make it happen.

* * *

"We want to work with you, but I had a conversation… a couple conversations yesterday and not everyone at AFC is on board with bringing you in for FUTURES." AUSA called a week ago with this disturbing news.

I inhale.

"Operations and other sections are glad you're engaged in this, but we're getting mixed messages."

Are you fucking kidding me right now?

I start pacing around my apartment like a caged animal.

"We want to work with you, and frankly you've been the most helpful out of anyone, but we need to know more about what happened."

"First, I appreciate this. I'm not surprised, but I am disappointed. As you said, I'm helpful, and I don't draw the same boundaries around work lanes as other people do. Gosh, I don't want that to sound cagey." I pause to take a breath. "I mean to say I'd rather just get the job done than worry about which lane I'm in when I do. Does that make sense?"

"It does. Okay, it sounded off because it's not consistent. Most people at AFC think very highly of you."

"Thank you for that. I'd encourage you to reach out to the Colonel and ask him. It's his shop, and if he thinks my presence would disrupt his team, he should be the one to make that call."

"You know, we mentioned that and were told he's really busy."

"What? He can't be too busy to manage his directorate and FUTURES is the big sha-bang this year in Austin. If AFC gets input at all in who you contract with, his level needs to be the one to give the thumbs up or thumbs down."

"Yeah, that feels right. We'll reach out and get back to you."

* * *

All the drama and he-said she-said stuff aside, I know you're wondering if I ate Splenda crusted peanut butter in front of AUSA leadership at their hotel in the morning. I refrained. I'm growing as a person.

I entourage into the gigantic conference room with AUSA. If you have to make an entrance under circumstances like these, that's probably the best way to do it. Almost everyone else is there, including the two people I'd put at the top of the "Most Likely to Throw Me Under a Bus" list.

I give each of them a pleasant "good morning" and eye contact. Eye contact is not held through the entire exchange. Roger that. There are lots of folks in the room to meet, though, so I busy myself being friendly.

AUSA's audio/visual contractor and their meeting/event contractor are seated together. I don't remember their names, but they were nice. Also, a couple FBI guys and the team from Continuum Interactive I brought in as a potential contractor for experiential events were there. They're Austin based and have a background in e-sports. This is the team who would execute on that little bitty promise I made to AUSA's president back in September.

After AUSA's lead, the senior-ranking person in the room, opened the meeting, she asks everyone to introduce themselves. The counterintelligence FBI guy and the supervisory FBI guy go first, and the woman next to me from Continuum Interactive shoots me the "what the hell?" eyes.

Civilians.

Later, on a break, I get a chance to say hello to the other two members of the Continuum Interactive team. They lead with the FBI question.

"Why is the FBI here?" asks the woman.

"I've never been in a room with an FBI agent," says the guy.

"No? Not even CI?" I kid.

"What is CI?" she asks the obvious follow up question.

"Counterintelligence." Their eyes are wide. "It's okay. We're proposing a public event to discuss the future of military weapons. Wouldn't you want the FBI to know who is trying to peek in the windows and why?"

That seems to calm them down even though it's slightly unsettling to think about. I failed to prep them on the FBI CI team. It never crossed my mind.

* * *

There were three days of meetings, site visits, breakfasts and lunches, and a trip to the interactive lab at University of Texas at Austin (UT) to see a demo of fun toys they could incorporate.

It was a lot. I am exhausted. At the end, though, 4:02 p.m., the team tells me they'll be signing the contract and moving forward with my services. Woohoo!

They jump in an Uber and leave me at the UT campus. I have a call at 5:00 p.m., who mistook the time zone and calls me an hour early. I push him off for a few minutes and let AUSA go to happy hour and dinner without me. I'm sure they needed quality team time.

I order my own ride home and call the guy back. This is a very loose connection. A friend of a friend of a friend, literally.

"Hi Robert, sorry about that."

"No Julie, my bad. I didn't pay close attention to the time zone. I'm on the train right now so this is a great time, thanks for calling back."

"Absolutely. I'm in a Lyft," we chuckle. Forget his name. From this moment on he will be referred to in this book as "Mr. Creepy."

CHAPTER 14

BUTT SNIFFING

———

The alpha male is always willing to walk away.

—ROOSH V

Last week, after returning from San Diego, I went to Capital Factory to visit AAL and met up with my friend Michael. As usual, he was running late. Someone always wants his time.

"Hey!" Downtown Randy Clark greets me with a big hug. "What are you doing here?"

"Waiting for Michael."

"He's here?"

"I freaking hope so," we laugh. Those special forces types have a way of disappearing on you. I'm positioned where I can see all the exits, so he can't leave without me catching him, if he's actually here.

"So," begins Randy, "I got this text and I don't know him or how to help."

Left field is my favorite place to pick flowers. Randy shows me the text. It's from a guy in D.C. looking to get a company into a pitch competition—classic startup. Except, this event is a collaboration between AAL and the Army Rapid

Capabilities and Critical Technologies Office (RCCTO). Wanting to jump into a government-funded pitch competition is common, but it doesn't work like this. They needed to apply months ago, go through the "down select" process, have all their tech reviewed in advance, and then receive an invite to the closed event.

Back to Randy and his text thread. How did the text get to him? He didn't know this guy. What is the tech? Turns out a former Secretary of the Navy gave the guy his number. Sure, that's a thing. All he had was a website and a vague description of their facial recognition software. Cool. Who doesn't want their face tracked by a machine?

I ask Randy to send me screenshots and connect me to the guy. I go back to killing time until Michael was ready by talking to BAE and an AAL lawyer, because that's how I spend my free time. My phone pings with the group text introduction between me and the random guy trying to get his client's company into the pitch competition, and I schedule time to connect.

This is how I end up in the back of a Lyft from UT to my apartment after AUSA leaves. I'm on a call with this guy about facial recognition and spoofing. Catch that? It's already level-five creepy to think my own face is following me around, it's another thing to think of what could happen if that data shadow wasn't real. Mr. Creepy wants to know if I know anyone who might be able to help his client enter the military marketplace, and if so, am I able to make that connection. Well, shoot, yes.

For the record, wouldn't Mr. Creepy already know if I did? Or his client? Just saying.

I explain to him the guy to meet is Michael and that I'll reach out. Since I'd just seen him, I knew he would be in town for the AAL/RCCTO event next week. It would take one text message to schedule a meet. I don't tell the guy I knew he'd be there. I don't know why, but sometimes I just like a bit of space.

I send that text to Michael. He writes back confirming he'll be in Austin. Cool. Would he be willing to meet a guy at the happy hour for the event? Sure. He hates that shit, but he was willing. Why? Why would "the guy" be willing to meet some random guy with a device in his pocket? Ah, now that's the question.

Everyone has a different answer. I could have asked the director of AAL, his deputy, any of the other folks, or maybe a tech buddy with knowledge of government procurement, and the "why" would have varied. Not that some would do it and others wouldn't. That's not the question here.

As for Michael, he gives a shit. He believes. He thinks what he's doing will help his buddies today and the guys/gals that come next. He's also resilient. He has gone nose to nose with the bureaucracy and keeps waking up to do it again. He's insane.

The other folks? Some would do it if they could leverage it as a win for their organization. I can't forecast that. Remember, all I have is a couple screenshots and a phone call. I can't tell them this thing is legit. They wouldn't take my word for it, anyway. Without specifics or independent validation, a lot of these guys won't take the meeting. Many are ego-driven and all give a shit, but some egos need more than others. That's why I don't trust everyone. A month ago, I made an introduction for a small company, and a member of the O-6 Rolodex ended up talking at the bar about all his prior work with a big defense program. He never asked how that company's technology could benefit the warfighter.

Other folks? The Michaels of the world? Their motivations are different. Aha! Look at that, I finally arrived at the real topic: motivation. I never worked for an intelligence agency. I was never trained by the government to assess and leverage someone's motivation for my own gain or that of my government. I'm just a regular girl who pays attention.

When someone asks how I feel about any of the people I've worked with I say, "I'm friendly with everyone, but I see everything." That's not true. I'm neither friendly with everyone nor aware of everything. I'm a bubbly extrovert, so I appear friendly. I have also spent years in the back of big meetings watching power move around. I love it. Move over football, I'm watching the power dynamics!

* * *

If power dynamics were a sport, I'd have a closet full of jerseys. Watching power bounce around a room is my spectator sport. I credit the State Department with helping me discover my love of power-watching. (I need to trademark this. I call dibs!)

Every week we had review meetings and I was the "slide jockey." I am not making that title up; it's a real thing. These were classified briefings in a classified conference room, so I'm skipping over a lot of details. There were meetings. There were egos. And there were teams. This pretty much describes every conference room in the D.C. metro area, right?

I was not personally invested in the outcome of the meetings. My role could easily have been handed off to one of the fifty-plus people who had to be in the room. I had no reason to be there except I found it fascinating, and the meetings were so painful to the folks who had to be there that my cheer was misinterpreted as genuine interest.

The only way I stayed awake and enjoyed them was because I was listening to a tennis announcer in my head. There was a judge, the tippity-top in the building, and the review booth occupied by the guy faithfully sitting next to me. We sat all the way in the back so he could nudge me, shift his feet, or clear his throat to indicate something wasn't right. He brought me chocolates and taught me how to read the bullshit. Best meetings ever.

I didn't know the phrase at the time—I have to credit this to an Army guy—but the behavior that had me hooked is affectionately called "butt sniffing." I'd heard rumblings internally that folks at AFC HQ felt disconnected from the mission. Okay, some of those rumblings were my own, and I admit it. In an effort to fix that feeling, I reached out to a guy I met at AUSA in 2018. He's a cool dude and a colonel, I think. I sent him a note on LinkedIn, and before the end of the day, AFC's PAO got a call from a very nice Sergeant First Class (SFC).

When AFC opened HQ in Austin, my job moved with it. I came down in January 2019 to see if I wanted to move with my job. The PAO Colonel and I had a real heart-to-heart.

"If I move here, I need space to run. Open the gate and let me work, sir," came out of my mouth. The man personifies Texas, so he understood what I wanted.

"You want to run? You can run here. There is more than enough work," he gestured out his window with a view of the State Capitol building. That was all I needed to hear. From that moment on, he affectionately called me Filly.

"Filly, phone," the PAO Colonel called out from a few cubes back.

I stared at his outstretched hand, waiting for me to take the call on the other line, on his phone no less. "What? Me? Does anyone even know I work here?" I respond.

He chuckled and handed me his phone.

I took it because when a colonel hands you something, you take it. "AFC this is Julie."

"Hi Julie, this is SFC so-and-so and I'm calling from the Cross Functional Team."

"Hi." I have no idea what's happening, and I just missed the guy's name. Is it obvious yet?

"The Colonel told me you were interested in a visit to display some of our tech at headquarters."

Oh, wow.

"Yes! Oh yes. Yes, I have this crazy idea to do a little show and tell."

"I can't come this week, but I can be there next week on Monday." He then described the eight or so things he'd be bringing. I have no idea what those are, and I have no authority to approve his travel. This is going to be awesome!

It wasn't the next Monday, but when he got to town, we had him stage his show and tell in our section. A couple guys from AAL popped over to see what he brought. One of them, an actual operator, picked up the most precious and most expensive prototype on display and started whacking it against the table.

I was horrified! SFC so-and-so didn't flinch. Later, I asked him what that was about, and he explained that during tech demos, the folks with the most experience in the harshest environments do that. They don't always whack expensive electronics against the hardest object within reach, but it is their role to break the prototype. It's not done to be mean;

it's done because it has to be done. If it gets to the operator and can't take a beating, it's useless.

"Butt sniffing" is the process of alpha dogs figuring out who is who and establishing dominance. In that room, as in probably any room that guy is in, he's the alpha of the alphas. Oh, how I love watching power dynamics.

* * *

Back to Michael. How did I get "the guy" to give some CEO I've never met the time of day? The time of his day? First, I'm not an asshole. Second, Michael knows my motivation. See that? He can read me—not in a "like attracts like" kind of way, but in a purely transparent way. He has been trained by those who know and has had to rely on those skills to keep his ass alive—and to keep other people alive. So, it's not hard to text Michael and get him to meet up. He knows my reasons and my hustle. He also knows I won't waste his time.

I caught up with Michael that day around 3:00 p.m. We weren't scheduled to meet the CEO guy for a couple hours. I'd had a few meetings already and was psycho-hungry. I was not hangry. Hangry is cute. I cuss out my Lyft driver (in my head) for taking the slowest route to AAL. It's going to be a long day.

I walk into the least opulent Omni hotel in the world and text him.

Me: I'm here.

Michael: Don't come up. I'll be down.

Eight minutes go by...

Me: I'm hungry.

Michael is a smart man, and he knows what hungry looks like on me. The clock had started. Eight more minutes go by, and I see him descend from the eighth floor in the glass elevator. He shakes his head at the sight of me. I'm sitting like a kid on an oversized planter box in the lobby eating mixed nuts I'd scavenged from Capital Factory.

* * *

Michael and I walk out and scavenge food for him, now that I've stabilized. He's one of those ridiculously muscled dudes who seems to eat and drink whatever, but he's probably very careful. I don't know how else someone could get that kind of mass.

We decide on CAVA. Awesome. I got a side of shredded chicken with a couple toppings out of solidarity. It would be rude to make the man eat alone, and I still had a few hours before we were meeting Mr. Creepy's client, Brett. I can't risk hangry twice in one day. I don't want to go to jail.

Michael and I catch up. He's a good dude. When I was in D.C., he and I worked on opposite sides of a pony-height cubicle wall. We have common ground. We also have a shared frustration regarding bureaucracy. Michael tries, but the deck is stacked against him.

Eventually, we finish our CAVA and head up to meet Brett to hear about the technology his company, Cubed, invented. He's standing in the lobby in his suit. In the first minute or two, Michael and Brett find their common ground and the conversation moves on without me. I was in heels and getting tired of balancing on the balls of my feet, so I suggested we move to an open table at the bar. We were eight flights below the happy hour we were scheduled to attend. It didn't matter. We spent two hours at that table. Michael asked questions. Brett answered them. Michael played with the tech.

I went home happy, and more freaked out by the creepy-ass tech than I thought I would be. The tech needed a proper review, a.k.a. more invasive butt sniffing, but I hadn't wasted Michael's time. That was the important thing.

CHAPTER 15

AM I GOING TO JAIL YET?

The difference between treason and patriotism is only a matter of dates.

—ALEXANDRE DUMAS

I'm a little disappointed. It just hit me that the only firm Valentine's Day plans I have with Andrew are happening right now. Both of us are working on our laptops at the Austin Central Library. He booked a room. How much should I read into the fact that he didn't get around to booking a table for dinner?

If I had nothing better to do, I'd overthink that, but right now my head is spinning. I just had brunch with a friend fluent in international trade law. I don't know where or how I meet these people, but this brunch was great timing.

I'm worried I've already fucked up. Like, we're in the treason zone on the felony chart. Brett's company has sold his facial recognition technology internationally, and my gut says this isn't right. The tech is too good. The International Traffic in Arms Regulations (ITARs) are pretty clear on this subject. So, how is he selling overseas and not in the US? We get pretty upset when Chinese students come to study in the US and send back notes about their research, but this is a real device with national security implications. I don't have enough information about ITARs and encryption keys, though.

I look up to see Andrew typing away totally productive and happy. I, on the other hand, am frozen. I'm too afraid to even google things on my laptop.

I grab my purse and get up. Andrew looks up and smiles.

"I'll be right back," I say in my sweet voice reserved for men occupying his position in my life. Boyfriends get the nice version of me. It isn't a standard feature; it's an upgrade, and there's a packet of paperwork and an approval process to get it installed.

I head straight for the laptop checkout kiosk. It's a thing. Two hours for free. Austin is awesome.

Do you know what I forgot to bring to the library today? My library card. I return to the room and ask if he has his card on him. Nope. He does have a photo of his, though.

I can't zoom in on the barcode quite right, so the kiosk won't let me have a laptop. I guess that's a good feature for preventing someone from using another person's card to check out a laptop and Google things they shouldn't. Ahem.

I'm fully aware I'm trying to hide my search history, which means I'm close to the wrong side of the ledger. How will I know if I'm breaking the law if I don't look it up? I'm sure as hell not going to look up library books on the subject and spend days reading about treason and trade. I'd much rather ask Google to figure out what I really need to know.

I inhale.

What if I just look up military sales and go from there? An hour later, I've learned that I need to talk to Brett. If they've sold this technology overseas, certainly someone from the Department of Commerce has given them an export license. Brett wants to work with me to sell his technology to our military, other agencies, and internationally, but until I know if I'm going to jail... we wait.

Luckily, there are plenty of other stressful things to focus on. How about building an outline for an event I want to host on the shoulder of FUTURES to establish my brand and show off all the cool tech I've encountered over the last... six weeks? Sure. Here's what I've got so far in the classic bureaucracy five Ws format, with the sixth bonus W:

- Who: Nontraditional companies with disruptive hardware to display for traditional defense contractors and interested government employees.

- What: An evening to bring the unknown to big players. It's glam and exclusive.

- When: June 23 (9:00 p.m.-midnight, but not during AUSA)

- Where: The Eleanor, Austin

- Why: Non-traditional companies need a platform where they can show off their products/services/technologies. This night is for the small companies with big ideas. Small companies with big impact hardware, because this is where innovation is happening. Ahem, where innovation has happened. While the government waits for the three or four times a year the R&D/SBIR window is open, there are companies making progress every day. Bad Uncle Sam.

- Wow: Velvet rope used to conceal a few items from industry and reveal other items.

If you haven't been paying attention to military modernization (gasp), here's a quick recap:

1. Recently, the Air Force has been investing in R&D through challenges and SBIRs. They've funded more companies faster than any other service.

2. There is tension between the people in charge of deciding what warfighters will need in the future, the current warfighters who are seemingly not paying any attention to their future capabilities, and the capitalist economy, where innovation drives like a NASCAR newbie (fast, can turn well, plays somewhat well with competition, but sometimes crashes). This tension is not good for business, or for the warfighters.

3. The current "requirements" system forces yesterday's warfighters to project what tomorrow's military will need. Some people... ahem... question why today's old white men are in charge of tomorrow's capabilities. It's not a dig on diversity but on ownership. The next generation doesn't own their capabilities. I think if they knew what was coming—what is here—they'd pay attention.

I want to create a venue where we talk about what's coming and what's here. Not about what the Army or other branches think they need or want, but about what exists. Lots of discussion happens around requirements and needing a problem to solve, but on some level we all know what the problems are. We know because society has the same problems at a larger scale, but their risks are different.

For example, I love my phone. It holds all my thoughts: when to wake up, what is happening in the news, songs to dance to in the morning, my emails, texts from Mr. Wonderful, which make me smile. I can check in for a flight, use GPS and navigation to get to the airport (or have Uber do it), and scan a mobile ticket to get on the plane… the list goes on.

Now, let's do this again as the warfighter. Their connected device (broadening this a bit) does everything mine does. Simple, right? They use GPS and navigation to get to their destinations, they connect with each other, they read email, play music, and check in on the news. The difference is in risk.

They have to balance expectations and consequences. For me, if my phone starts acting up, I give it a nasty look, close the app, and open it back up again. If it doesn't wake me up, it's almost a guarantee I made a mistake. If my playlist loses signal in a dead zone, I just get frustrated. If the GPS reroutes my Uber, it's because of traffic, and the app is just taking good care of me. Thanks, Uber!

For warfighters, if their device goes through a dead zone, it's a literal dead zone. See the difference? If the GPS reroutes their ride, how do they know someone hasn't hacked in and spoofed the route with a destination that'll lead them into a trap? Their expectations are different. Their consequences are different. They accept this risk for the same noble sheepdog reason that I admire them for.

Now, what is happening in the background to ensure the warfighters don't lose connectivity or trust in their GPS? Good question. First, it's the military. They have redundancies and options to prevent a catastrophic loss of connectivity. They also train for that scenario. Second, and speaking from my experience with the Army, they have entire organizations dedicated to knowing what gaps exist and navigating through them. These gaps are identified and sometimes they're addressed in future capability sets (years out, like right now they're looking at 2023). Sometimes they're not. These gaps are widely reported in the press, at the unclassified level.

Here's the real issue buried deep in this text: there are companies in this country today that have bridged those gaps that cannot find a way to tell the military about it. Even if they could... even if they could stand by the cupcake pop-up shop in the Pentagon and hand out their solutions, it won't get to the front lines.

Insane, right? There are solutions already, but we're stuck. It's like neighbors who speak different languages and can see the other one could really use their spare kiddie pool on a hot day, but they can't seem to get it over the fence. It's madness.

There was a time when I joked about writing a letter at the end of the day to the warfighter explaining how I failed them. Sarcasm can soothe the soul.

Dear Warfighter,

Super sorry I wasn't able to get that company a table at the event. Turns out, they presented at one six months ago and the event organizers want to see new stuff. So, even though you needed this six months ago, I don't think it's coming. But hey, good luck out there tonight!

Love,

Julie

One day, at one of those big events, I realized I was done supporting this system. My heart is still with the mission—with the warfighters—but my head wanted a chance to deliver.

So, here I am on this adventure trying to create my own event. Oh, the irony.

* * *

Yay! Library time is over. I feel like I lost ten pounds getting those thoughts out of my head and onto the screen. Coincidentally, I remembered I know a consultant who does trade compliance and was in the Navy. He'll tell me if I'm breaking the law by consulting with Brett's facial recognition company, Cubed, and all it'll cost me is my pride.

Cha-Ching!

Time to see what Andrew has in store for Valentine's Day…

* * *

I've got to get to the bottom of this international arms dealing thing. Is Brett selling military products to other countries? If he is... I'll be publishing this book from prison. If our government has determined he is not selling weapons-grade technology to foreign governments, then I'll proceed. Why? Because this is the type of product that will save warfighter lives.

That's a lot of pressure to put on a coffee meeting. Luckily, it's at The Line, a gorgeous boutique hotel in downtown Austin. I do everything I can to get as close to hotel breakfast as possible, and this one comes with white tablecloths and proper napkins.

Brett is late. He is always late, and today he is blowing in hot.

"What have you got for me?" he asks as he sits down.

"Hello. Well, I have questions."

That stops his momentum cold. This Bulgari-clad CEO doesn't like to be questioned.

"I need to understand how the product is sold overseas. If you're trying to sell it to our military, then you should know they won't like that other countries have this capability."

"I don't understand. I've already sold it to parts of other governments."

"Yes," I said he came in hot, right? "Did you get an export license or go through ITARs?" I ask.

"We did all that already. I don't understand what you want."

Slowly I tell him, "I want to know that selling this overseas didn't violate any US laws, Brett."

"I said we got an export license. The FBI came by and looked at our paperwork. I hired a top New York law firm. What's the concern?"

I inhale.

"My concern is that I need to do my own due diligence. You're asking me to broker sales with the USG and other countries. I'm not going to do either until I have assurance I'm not breaking any laws and you haven't either."

I wish I could tell you the conversation improved, but it didn't. Brett doesn't see the concern; he just sees the money.

"If you get me the meetings with the military, you'll get a cut of each sale."

"I know. I saw the agreement."

"You didn't sign it."

"No, I didn't, and I won't until I know you're playing by the rules. I've had a security clearance for half a dozen years, Brett, so I take treason pretty fucking seriously."

"Treason? This isn't treason! I'm a patriot. That's why I built this technology."

What a weird label to put on yourself. It works when you say it about someone who has done great things for their country. It doesn't work when you use it to gloss over how you're really just trying to recoup investor money.

"Brett, are you able to provide me with a copy of the export license and the FBI's determination on the ITARs classification?" Look at me throwing big acronyms around!

"I don't know why I need to give them to you, but yes. I can do that."

Oh my god, why was that so hard?

"Great. Now, let's talk strategy for the US military. I realize the product is commercially available, but they will want something special. It'll have to be ruggedized."

He pops his top. "It's fine the way it is! They don't need anything else done to it."

If this was a phone call, I could hang up and pretend I lost connection. It's harder to pull off, "I'm about to go through a tunnel... I'll call back if I lose you...," in person. It could be done, and this conversation is on my top three list of opportunities to try it.

I inhale.

I was a nanny one summer a few years ago, so I summon my nanny voice and respond. "Yes, it is fine. It has a great capability, but in order for the Army to use it, they will want it to be able to survive in different scenarios. They make those rules, I don't."

"What kind of scenarios?"

"It has to live in every climate, through all sorts of abuse, and still be reliable. The good news is that the military has pockets of R&D money to help disruptive technology transfer from a commercial product to a military one."

"How do we do that?"

If I knew, I'd be the Duchess of the Pentagon. "I'm happy to connect you to consultants who do that, but it is outside my area of expertise. I wouldn't want to lead you astray."

"How much will that cost me? This is all very expensive, Julie. I already spent five million dollars on marketing."

Not my problem, and you're an idiot.

"We'll have to negotiate. It can be a percentage or a flat fee, but the funding is graduated. For a SBIR Phase 1, the maximum is fifty thousand dollars."

"Fifty thousand dollars? That won't be enough money. You need to think of something else."

I smirk and blink slowly, allowing him to settle. "No, I don't. This is an option I'm presenting you with. That's all. If you'd like to continue the conversation with an SBIR consultant, that can be arranged." I'm as frustrated with the need for another consultant as he is. Why are SBIRs so complicated?

"I'll let you know," he says as he grabs his Louis Vuitton wallet and pulls out the valet ticket. Uh huh.

Dear Warfighter,

Hey, how's war? I'm good. Just had a meeting with a defense entrepreneur. I don't think he's going to make it through the government contracting gauntlet to hand over some creepy facial recognition tech to you. He's just not cut out for this business.

Anyway, good luck out there!

Love,

Julie

CHAPTER 16

RELATIONSHIPS

If you can connect people, you can create the future.
—SCOTT HEIFERMAN

This just happened. I was waiting with my friend Ann to get on a plane to Cabo and a call I was hoping to have before I went into airplane mode for three days came in. It was Danny, the guy who connected me with Heather and ultimately launched me off on the San Diego wild goose chase for Nina. He's also the guy in D.C. who schooled me on the practice of human intelligence (HUMINT). HUMINT is the collection of information from humans. When information is analyzed or combined with other information sources, it becomes intelligence.

The lessons took place where you'd expect them to: at an old cop bar in a D.C. suburb. We developed a routine. The first one to the bar ordered two plates of wings, with ranch, and by the time the check came he'd have tossed back a dozen pints. I can't smell Old Bay seasoning without thinking of him. We met as potential colleagues, but I thought of him as a friend. It's easy to second guess if we were friends because I was in the hands of a trained handler. Eventually, we started playing a little game. No name, but the objective was to read the body language of the other patrons. He trained me to see patterns in relationships and note when those patterns change. Hence why he was one of the lucky ones to help me pick up the pieces of my shattered heart when things ended with Hal. We worked backwards to find the moment when our patterns changed. He wasn't there for a *Sex and the City*-esque relationship dissection over mimosa brunch, he was there to teach me something. It was an academic exercise.

So why is Danny calling? I sent him two texts a few hours ago. I know he barely looks at his phone during the day, and I also know it's a burner. D.C. can be so weird sometimes.

The message I sent read, "This is legit. Who do you know who may be interested?" I also included a link to the company's website. That's it. If there was anything between the website and his network, he'd tell me.

Now, it's important to know that Danny is an enigma. Pre-9/11 he enlisted in the infantry and became a sniper. I think it was an injury that caused him to reclassify into military intelligence, but I don't know for sure. I do know he was a HUMINT handler in the Army, and in that chapter, he suffered a traumatic brain injury. Danny was medically discharged.

When his brain healed, it made him a savant. The man sleeps maybe two hours a night, is constantly playing chess in his head, and remembers everything before his accident. It's spooky. He's also dying very quickly. In a couple years his brain, still accelerating, will fail to keep his body alive.

For now, he puts it to use as Artifio's chief data officer delivering on contracts for the US IC, a few allies, and a couple nonprofits. When we nearly worked together a year and a half ago, that deal is the same one that Matt in San Diego was working. It's all connected, right?

I was supposed to go with Danny to Africa to help promote the company. Why would I have to go all the way to Africa to do that? Well, their core business is patriotic but not publicly releasable. Luckily, they work with nonprofits in a few countries to help track poachers and endangered species. If we could promote these stories, we could demonstrate their capabilities in an unclassified environment.

The security software doesn't care if the person it's tracking is trafficking rhino horns or drugs. A bad guy is a bad guy. So, Danny is in high demand. When I was working on that proposal with Matt, he was constantly traveling to NATO countries—and Sweden.

I'd just spent a few hours at the bar of the Centurion Lounge with Ann. We were a little buzzed—her from wine and me from Americanos. Everyone is #winning. Since she will board in a lower group (ahem, higher... this is airline hierarchy), I take the call. It's not rude in our friendship because I know she will board without me in a second and leave me waiting for my group. This girl has ditched me at airport security several times to go through her TSA pre-check line. Then, she waits for me on the other side. We operate with a unique set of friendship rules, but they work for us.

After just a few minutes on the call, Danny had recapped what was interesting to him on the Cubed site: advanced tactical facial recognition. Then he asked, "What do you want?" I knew that question was coming. My answer was simple: to know if he thought anyone he knew would be interested.

That question used to trip me up. How do you say, "I want you to introduce me to the CIO of a foreign government so I can make money off the sale of clandestine facial recognition software," without laughing? Specifically, at gate A2 in Phoenix.

That's the difference between can and do. He can. He absolutely can do that with one email, maybe two. So how does he cross the line from can to do? What do I need to tell him to convince him to help me? And why would he? He doesn't have to do a thing. He can say what others may say, "blah blah blah I don't believe this is worth me putting my reputation on the line for." They don't actually say that. They say, "this would be really interesting if you can get it validated." Pansies.

Answer: earlier in the conversation he revealed what he wanted. Very simply he said he wanted to know more about how the tech worked. How is it processing the data? What network? That's all. Danny wants knowledge.

So, what did I say? "I want to know if you think anyone you've met along the way would be interested. And if so, to open that door." Folks... that's the truth. It's so powerful, especially in this business.

"I'll connect you to Alexander." Then the conversation gets muddled as nearby gate agents start making announcements. What did he say about Alexander? Who the hell is Alexander? I'm asking follow up questions and that's when I say, "Oh he's the J2 of Sweden. In Sweden. Got it. Okay, when is your next trip?" I look at Ann, who hasn't ditched me yet and is laughing her head off. She knows I just took a phone call that opened up Sweden, and hopefully NATO, to a capability our own military is too cumbersome to get their hands on.

How does she know? I'd just told her the story of Valentine's Day. We were sitting at the bar catching up and she howled when I got to the part where I realized if this tech were to be weaponized, then I am basically an international arms dealer. She never doubted it or questioned me. She just laughed at how ridiculous my world is. One minute I'm trying to convince a seasoned executive to invest a few grand in a thought leader campaign on LinkedIn (exactly what he wanted but clearly didn't want to pay for), and the next I'm on the phone surrounded by Cabo-goers one step away from a meeting with the CIO of Sweden's military. Yeah, if you're not laughing, you're not paying attention.

I can't make this shit up. I'm typing this out from seat 25D waiting for the nice person to hand me a Diet Coke that will make me have to pee on the hour trip from the airport to Cabo San Lucas. Or worse, on the journey to the Four Seasons. No, I'm not paying. Ann won an award at her pharmaceutical company, so in the middle of this conversation about enabling creepy-ass facial recognition spoofing, I'm en route to an all-inclusive trip to Mexico paid by legal drug money. Oh! And before Danny called, I was deciding whether it was worth it to fly back from Mexico on Sunday, arrive at 6:00 p.m. in Austin, and turn around on the 6:00 a.m. flight out to Sao Paulo to have dinner with my friend Inacio.

Why? Why would I spend a grand of my own money to fly to Brazil for dinner? Ahh, that is another good question. Here's one more: why didn't I bring any Modafinil pills? Those would be nice right now. You should ask your doctor about Modafinil or watch the movie *Limitless*.

Same answer: because I can and do, and so does Inacio. He can. He can do a lot of things. One of them is to help me get Cubed into the country, now that Brett has proven he has Uncle Sam's authorization to sell his tech overseas. He can also help me get into other NGOs and Concordia. It's not that he can. He's a doer. He has keys to all the doors, and since I've never asked him for anything, he trusts me.

That is important. Inacio is a busy guy co-running a multi-national company, competing in Formula 1 racing, and who's well connected.

Yep.

How do I know him? How am I able to send that guy a WhatsApp and have him agree to dinner?

This theme repeats: because he trusts me, and I have never asked for anything. If I was short sided, I would ask Cubed to pay for my trip and make an introduction, but that is using him for his connections. I can't do that. I don't do that.

Instead, and as subtle as this difference is, I will fly down to have dinner with my friend. I'll end up telling him about my new company and the clients I now represent. At that point, he can decide if he wants to know more or what doors he can open. Just because he has the keys in no way means he has any obligation to let me drive the metaphorical racecar.

It's the same thing with Danny except Danny asked what I wanted. If Inacio asked me, I'd tell him: to pick his brain about exporting to Brazil. It's the truth. If I was only in it for Cubed, I'd blow this opportunity because they aren't paying for the trip. But I'm not. I know from my gut that missing out on dinner means missing out on being in the room when lightning strikes.

The last time I listened to my intuition and got on a plane, I went from Austin to Saint George to Vegas to San Diego and back to Austin. I met three companies I'm going to put front and center at my event, Conceal::Reveal, on the shoulder of FUTURES. How many connections could come from flying to Sao Paulo? Well, I'll be keeping one fresh, and then I can come back in a few weeks to follow up on those ideas.

It's like when people say, "you have to spend money to make money." Those fuckers aren't spending their own money. If this was someone else's money I'd gladly tell them this was a quick trip that isn't justifiable in dollars. The true currency here is the relationship.

But… that doesn't change the fact that I'm paying my AmEx every month with my own money. Today is Thursday. Dinner is Monday.

Onward to Mexico!

CHAPTER 17

I NEED A NAP
(AND A HUG)

———

There are only the pursued, the pursuing, the busy and the tired.
—F. SCOTT FITZGERALD

It's so kind of February to give me an extra day. What a week! I flew back from Sao Paulo on Wednesday, grabbed a manicure at the Miami Centurion Lounge and lunch (I'm deducting thirty dollars from the annual fee in value earned), and went straight from the Austin airport to a ninety-minute massage.

I'm a flipping baller.

I chased that day with two meetings on Thursday and a hot date with Andrew. Friday was piled high with more coffee meetings than I could drink, and now I'm back at the Austin airport and it's only Saturday morning. Whew. I took a nice walk this morning to ground myself before I had to start pulling my luggage around again.

Tonight, I'll rest my head at some Marriott in Arlington near AUSA's headquarters. We're working on Sunday because I'm in a graduate certificate program at Georgetown University from Monday through Wednesday. Yay me. This trip is twice as packed as the first one in January, but it'll be twice as good. [wink]

* * *

Ten hours. Ten. Hours.

We talked, white-boarded, planned, and strategized. We troubleshooted the flaming hoops of bureaucracy, twice. In my experience, AUSA operates with the hierarchy of the Army, and I attribute that culture to the leadership. They are retired Army. It only makes sense that the Army's association, run by prior officers and NCOs, mirrors the Army.

Except, they have less traditional hierarchy folks just a rung or two down the ladder. Those folks are fun. This day flew by, but it was a long one. I'll keep mum on what we planned for FUTURES because I want you to be surprised.

* * *

By the time I got my luggage and reached my darling ex's apartment last night, it was late. Edward left the air mattress and sheets out for me in the second bedroom, but he was nowhere to be found. Classic Edward.

Today was a lot. I knew the route to campus from when I got my executive master's degree there. That annex is located just north of the Chinatown metro. It's also the Verizon Center metro. I know it as the one metro stop, but I've never managed to exit where I wanted or thought I was. Never. I always pop out at the wrong place.

I was sad my favorite French store was closed. When did we start closing Maison Kayser stores? Window displays with macaroons used to fill me with joy.

I don't know what to think about this program I'm in. It's a certificate in facilitation, which I hope will take me from spectator to athlete in my favorite sport: power dynamics. I'm not sure that's where I'll end up, though. The rest of the cohort is focused on being facilitators—shocking, I know—but I just want to learn how to shift the energy in a room.

Oh well, Uncle Sam is paying, and it's a good enough reason to get me to D.C. once a month monthly through June.

* * *

That little shit. I tried to set up a dinner or happy hour with Edward and Heather, because I think they should meet, and he countered with an invite to some lobbyist event tonight. I'm always down for free food, but I really want to get those two in the same room.

I didn't see Edward last night, and today all I've received are instructions to meet him at the L2 Lounge. No visitor's entrance at the State Department—the Harry S. Truman Building (HST) —for me this trip. I never felt like I belonged there in the past, even though I was a badge-wearing contractor for three years. It was as if they could spot me as a nobody. I mean, how many times did I walk into that building and a literal red carpet was out front with real dignitaries and entourages of bodyguards? Pretty much every time.

I only ever went through the visitor's entrance on my first day, so I'm glad Edward decided to skip that exercise.

Knowing me, I would go to the wrong security guard and screw up the screening. I can just see Edward standing on the other side watching me. His face would say, "wow, how does she function in society?"

HST is confusing, much like the Pentagon. I'm glad we're rendezvousing at a private club instead. Remember how I started today by exiting out the wrong, clearly marked metro exit? It's a much more civilized experience as a guest at L2. This time my guide, wearing a beautiful suit, breezes me through to the parking lot to meet Edward. We're not staying. Then he drives us to the valet at the Congressional Country Club. Why not?

Okay, so I read the entire situation wrong, but thankfully I was appropriately attired. I'd snuck heels into my bag and wore a long black dress to class. I also had a shawl (not cashmere or pashmina, just a cheap-ass soft gray wrap), so I was good to go just about anywhere in this town. When in doubt, dress like you came from somewhere better. Don't give the usual line about how you're going somewhere better later, but act like you already were. It's power dynamics with dress-up clothes. God, I love this town.

The location feels right. There are two women in the ballroom and a bazillion white men. I turn to Edward as we approach and say, "where are the women?"

He turns and says, "what do you mean? I see one now!" Classic Edward humor. Thanks, dude.

I meet one, and she was lovely. There are also a couple hundred dudes—lawyers, from the look of the suits. This was not a lobbyist thing, though, and everyone knew my name. That's weird, right? "Oh, you're Julie." What? I am, yes... but wait, why am I here?

I met Edward a long time ago when he briefed a meeting I was in on his signature program. I repeated the story many times that night, once I realized that I was seated at table one with the CEO of the organization honoring Edward for his commitment and service.

Classic Edward, again! He just plopped me into the situation. He loves this. Surprising people and watching them move through the situation is his game. I figured out my role tonight was the supportive female charmer. He knew I could handle it, and that I'd get whatever I wanted out of it.

Tonight, I want dessert. I charm the chocolate petal ice cream out of the guy two seats down from me after finishing my own. Mission accomplished.

Edward receives an award, and we celebrate his photo spread in a magazine. Sometimes I forget he's a pretty big deal, but not tonight. Between courses, of which there were many, he checks and re-checks his phone. COVID-19 was starting to get coverage, and the man who never stops working was… working.

* * *

By the end of our final day of class in D.C. on Wednesday I am exhausted. I hadn't seen Edward since I abandoned him Monday night. Once we get back to his place, he turns on the television, and I build myself a beanbag nest on the floor. I pass out watching *Star Trek: Picard*.

I pick a fight with Andrew tonight. I'm not proud of it, but it was coming. I'm sick, and I feel awful. Everything I see is COVID-19 related, and I'm in deep denial. I text him that I felt sick and exhausted, and he came back with a photo of him getting pizza. I need him to give more of a fuck.

So, I think we broke up during our first and only fight.

I don't need him to hold my hand, but it would be great if he'd responded to my text about feeling sick during a pandemic with a follow-up question. I don't know how to explain to him he needs to be in my corner. Being an entrepreneur is insane, and I know I've got the tough female thing going, but I really just want a man who can look me in the eye and ask, "You good?"

The end.

* * *

In case you are wondering what it's like to go through a breakup while staying at your ex's, I have news for you; it's pretty great. I didn't see Edward until two days later, after which I had been to Whole Foods at least three times and could hide the empty ice cream pints. I left one in his freezer half-eaten. He won't touch it. He knows better.

I highly recommend this scenario. For one, the person I'm staying with cares about me. He's never home, and when I finally saw him again and told him Andrew and I broke up, his response was, "Why didn't you tell me? I would have come home." He would've come home with a potential global pandemic raining down on the world and while working insane hours at the State Department.

Let that sink in. That's exactly what I'm looking for in a partner. In case you're interested in the position, please send your application packet to Edward.

CHAPTER 18

THE RUSSIANS

—

Pay attention to your enemies, for they are the first to discover your mistakes.

—ANTISTHENES

The ninety-nineth day of my company passed without me knowing, which means the one-hundredth day did, too. That's fine. I would have used it as an excuse to buy DEFIANT a cake. It was just two days after breaking up with Andrew, so cake would have gone well with all the ice cream I ate... a missed opportunity.

Even though I didn't know it was the ninety-nineth day doesn't diminish what happened. Day ninety-nine, the ninety-nineth, niner-niner... I don't know what to call it yet, but it was the first day I know of, with confirmation, that Russian intelligence (specifically the GRU) knows I exist. So, for ninety-eight days I was blissfully unaware that a foreign intelligence service cared about my little company and her little attempt at subverting their work.

What happened on the ninety-nineth day? How about we focus on what happened on the one-hundred-and-first.

You see, it's all a big game when you're working on the inside of the bureaucracy. There are people who try to keep you safe, people who monitor things, people who pay attention... it's lovely. There are even people you report weird things to, like that time the guy on the train platform outside Tel Aviv tried to dig a little too deep for a casual conversation... or the two guys who tag-team followed me in Amman. I had people I could tell—people I had to tell, or else I'd be in really big trouble.

Now, I don't have people. I have my gut. But between you, me, and the lamppost, no one cares what my gut says now until I'm floating in a lake, or, until I've broken the law. Say, for example, I'm approached by someone and asked to introduce a company to a buyer in our military... wait, that happened.

How about if I fly overseas to discuss technology with a foreign government... wait, that happened.

Okay, how about I'm blackmailed into doing something because a foreign government thinks I'm compromised, and they have leverage. It's a classic Netflix movie plot, right? That last one hasn't happened, yet.

For now, we wait. Either I eff up or they get tired of watching. How do I even know that day ninety-nine was "the day" I hit their radar? I invited someone to a meeting, and that individual was contacted by Russian intelligence, as confirmed by the USG, who kindly told this guy they'd like to meet when he was in Alexandria on Monday.

Alexandria on Monday, huh? How interesting, since I'm the person this guy is meeting. Who is this guy? Mr. Creepy himself. Remember the guy who introduced me to Brett and his tactical facial recognition software?

Meeting little old me is less about DEFIANT than it is about Mr. Creepy. He's a much bigger target than I am. Do you know what bothers me about that?

This fool ran the contact through the USG and still came to the meeting without telling me until we were in the middle of our meeting.

Not cool.

Now for the real question: would I have cancelled?

Nope.

Not because of any good reason, just because I'd enjoy the game for a few minutes before the stomach acid in my belly ate right through me and I ended up in the hospital. Stress is a bitch.

Now I have to wonder if the guy at the corner of the empty bar (ahem, empty) seated near us was listening. He was, but maybe he was listening because he was supposed to be, not because we were way more interesting than the void of nothingness that stretched before him.

Just another day in the beltway. Except, this one was not part of my original plan. I changed my flight to be there because Brett, Cubed CEO, asked me to. He wanted me at a meeting brought to you by the letter C: chief innovation officer (CIO), chief information security officer (CISO), chief security officer (CSO), chief technology officer (CTO)... These Cs and a handful of deputies (Ds) were from one of those big bureaucracies.

For a girl who spent six years in the city, this was huge. I know, they're just dudes (fact: all dudes) wearing American flag pins on their lapels and renting their brains to Uncle Sam for the good of the country. Brett briefed them on Cubed and his technology. As far as power dynamics goes, this was the closest I've ever been to the Olympics.

After the meeting, we walked around the Capital and took a handful of photos. Brett claimed they were for his kids, but I think this was as big of a deal for him as it was for me. It's not every day you get to be at the table when the USG's smarty-pants brigade gets to see something new.

Later, after Mr. Creepy let us know he'd been contacted by the GRU, Brett and I boarded a plane together to Austin. I was shaken. Am I the weakest link? Are they already in my systems? Are they in his? Is this one of those, "it's not you, it's me" moments? If either he or I are the reason the GRU knew about the meeting, then they already know about other meetings and the technology behind them.

Everything feels like it is duct-taped together. At the end of the day, we're on the plane, and Brett is completely passed out two seats away from me.

How fascinating! Did he understand the implications of that bit of information? Mr. Creepy dropped it in passing and laughed. In my experience, this isn't chuckle-worthy. Someone's Google calendar has been compromised, and these fools act like this is another day in the life of the D.C. elite.

Speaking of elite, just a minute ago Brett was popping gobstoppers and pistachios while watching a movie on his iPad. Poof! I look back and the man is asleep. He looks so human. These people, these men (all men), are sometimes so childlike and vulnerable. It's a nice reminder that not only are they people, but they're fallible little creatures.

* * *

It's 3:37 a.m., and I can't sleep.

It's way too flipping early to call it an "early start." I really want to go to yoga at nine... but I took that delicious melatonin at 10:00 p.m., and now it's too late to take more. I refuse to get out of bed or turn the light on and forfeit. Instead, my sleepy little brain is running through yesterday, the one-hundred-and-first day.

What annoys me about Mr. Creepy at the meeting yesterday in D.C. is the lack of warning. I'm used to men protecting me. He should have warned the rest of us we were likely under some sort of surveillance before we all showed up. OPSEC matters. Maybe something bigger is going on. I don't know.

Maybe I'm being oversensitive and reading too much into this, like it's the beginning of one of my dad's bedtime stories. I accept those activities as part of my world, part of our world. What I don't accept is being blasé about it.

Speaking of blasé, do you have any idea what time it is now?

PART 4

COVID-19

CHAPTER 19

NO SHADOW

———

The eye is always caught by light, but shadows have more to say.
—GREGORY MAGUIRE

This has been a wild week. I fly back on Monday with Brett and somehow, the week disappears. Today, I have three coffee meetings and a lunch that ends up switching to happy hour, and it is all sorts of wonderful. I love my life! However, I really need to go to Trader Joe's, but I'm afraid it's going to be a disaster.

President Trump announces a state of emergency, or national disaster, or whatever we are calling COVID-19 today. I'd seen photos of empty shelves at Trader Joe's across the country, so I figure I'll just walk by on my way home from work. If it was total madness, I'd appreciate it for the experience as is and not go in.

I live in a beautiful, modern condo in downtown Austin. I don't own it and couldn't afford to, but somehow, I can afford to rent it. Yay. One of the perks, in addition to a very low electricity bill courtesy of new construction, is having Trader Joe's in my backyard. It was zero effort to swing past.

I head home from meeting friends at a beautiful bar where a few of us gathered to have drinks to celebrate a special moment. Our friend had just put in her two weeks' notice as a contractor at AFC. Yay! So, we went out to celebrate and chose Perry's. If you're not familiar with the magic of Perry's on Fridays, it's famous for an enormous (three "ribs" high) and consistently perfect pork chop for sixteen dollars. Did I need a pork chop at 3:30 p.m.? Nope.

So, there I was walking home gently swinging half a giant pork chop in the telltale Perry's takeout bag like I didn't have a care in the world. The same little voice in my head who thought eating half the pork chop was a great idea said, "We should stop by Trader Joe's. Walk down third street. Do it." As I approach the store, I stop to talk to my second favorite security guard. He's lovely, but he's not Albert. Albert is an amalgamation of Tony Robbins and Pierce Brosnan. He's also super nice. Look, I'm there every other day, so these guys know way too much about me. Think about it. Maybe they're actually the GRU...

"How bad is it? I've seen things on twitter today," I said.

"We've been out of toilet paper since 10:00 a.m.! Look at the frozen section," not-Albert exclaimed.

"Oh wow. But you still have bottled water?" We were standing by a pallet stacked at least up to my waist. I lived on Oahu for eight years. Water, toilet paper, and protein bars were always the first things to disappear whenever the weather turned.

"Just this pile," not-Albert said.

Feeling the hysteria overtake me, I told not-Albert and other-not-Albert I would grab some, but there's no way I'd be able to carry it home. Where is Albert?

"Take the cart. Seriously. People do that all the time. We find them all over town," not-Albert said.

Oh wow. I mean, I can see my building through the sliding doors. I could do this. So, I walk around the store and buy salad, fresh asparagus, some beef, tons of coffee (tons), and chocolate (also tons). If I have to hunker down and trade—if this thing goes full *Bird Box*—imagine what I could get for a chocolate bar!

I reach the end of my binge shopping with a big old cart of "the essentials," and my phone rings. It's my lawyer, Shawn! He was supposed to be my third coffee meeting but was overtaken by his schedule, so I subbed in the pork chop. "J Dub!" Yeah, my lawyer has a nickname for me. That's totally normal.

"J Dub! I saw you strutting down the street. Where were you going? How did you not hear me yell your name out the window?"

"Cardi B."

"That explains the strutting. You walk like you have no shadow. Where were you going?"

"Home, by way of Trader Joe's. I'm in line with my cart of chocolate and coffee," I admit. It's my lawyer, you know? Honestly, he's more than that. He's my guidepost—my compass for what is ethical and what is not at all okay. He's the person who stands between me being a modern-day arms dealer and going to jail.

I begin to tell him all about the Conceal::Reveal event I'm planning in June. I tell him AUSA said I wouldn't be conflicting with their event and was good to go.

"Here's my concern, Shawn. I know booze is a big draw, but I don't know how to buy booze for the govvies and the military."

If you're not keenly aware of the catastrophic consequences of plying the government with booze, read a history book. Or, read up on what happened to AFWERX last year when a contractor held an event on the shoulder of their conference and served booze. The Pentagon put AFWERX on a tactical pause for months. This literally stalled innovation and modernization. It's a perfect "Dear Warfighter" post.

Dear Warfighter,

I hope war is going well. Super sorry we weren't able to award money to companies with disruptive tech; it would totally have helped you out. There was booze at an event, and the Pentagon lost their minds.

So, we're on a tactical pause.

Looking forward to helping you out in a few months.

Love,

The Bureaucracy

It's not that you can't buy them alcohol. Alcohol is everywhere. The attendees would be of legal age, of course, and I only plan to invite a handful. Why? My company is buying, and I'm a cheapskate. The thing to be aware of is the magic value threshold of the exchange. If there is any possibility that a government employee may be seen accepting a gift over the limit (twenty dollars per gift, capped at fifty dollars per year) they won't come. So, I needed Shawn to help me keep Conceal::Reveal clean.

"So, here's what you need to do, J Dub. Have two events. One with certain hours before the open bar where gov/mil employees can purchase their own drinks and look around. Then, they can disappear at 6:59 p.m. before the clock strikes 7:00 p.m. and the open bar starts. Invite any contractors or innovators you want from seven o'clock on."

And that's how we keep it clean. My goal for the event is to have a glamorous show and tell, not to ply government representatives with booze.

Then Shawn did what Shawn does best: he put it all in context again. "Remember, all of these guys have shadows. They run scared that any little thing they do, within the lines or outside of them, can cast a long shadow. You have no shadow now, and that terrifies them. Give them a safe place. Put the ethics out front so everyone knows you're playing their game. Then, when the clock strikes seven o'clock, you can show them what not having a shadow looks like as you kick them out."

We laugh. This is why Shawn is my lawyer. He gets me.

* * *

Welcome back to my bedroom. The current time is 3:26 a.m. I've been trying to fall back to sleep since 1:44 a.m. This is just great. Apparently, this is the week of not sleeping.

I have an idea! Let's play a little game.

I'll toss out a thought, and then we can overthink it until another one pops up. Starting with… how ridiculous it is that I tell people exactly how old my business is like it's a newborn baby.

"Oh, DEFIANT? She is two months and two weeks old today. She's still wearing her little newborn onesies."

I don't say that thing about the onesies. That'd be preposterous. Maybe someone stuck batteries in my biological clock? Nah, I do this because she was born on New Year's Day. It's just easy math. Also, I follow it up by saying, "My beautiful baby keeps me up at night. She's the only thing I think about. She's the thing I want to spend time with. I want to put one of those big flower bows on her head and plaster her all over Instagram."

I don't say that. Of course, she belongs on Instagram with a giant flower on the top right of her forehead. I just don't say it because 'irrational' is a label I don't think would be good optics right now. I definitely tell her she's the only thing that matters to me. She knows Mommy loves her. And... that is not a rational thought. This game is going really well.

I wish I was asleep.

Here I am. Here we are. It's 3:30 a.m. now. My darling baby is crying, and I don't know what I need to do to make her stop. Too much baby analogy to maintain... especially in the wee hours of the night. (I had to put one more pun in.) So, I guess I'll drop the baby thing for a little while. Can't do that with a real one, huh? Two points for the business baby analogy!

One of the biggest things on my mind right now, amid the mounting panic over COVID-19, is finding boundaries in this book. Where is the line between my personal and professional life when they're just parts of my day? I like my privacy. There are people in my life who like how private I am. Unfortunately, there are parts of my private life I think are relevant because I want you, dear reader, to understand the whole picture. As I tell people about the book, I usually start with, "It's the part of the Venn diagram that overlaps between a female entrepreneur and military modernization."

It's the overlap but not in a redundant way. Redundancy is frowned upon in federal spending yet held in high esteem in the military.

The "female entrepreneur lens" is wackadoodle. It's what makes viewing military modernization interesting; I think. We'll know if anyone else thinks that's the interesting part when this is published. This is a complicated space to be because, despite how private I've been, I don't want to tell the story sanitized.

For example, tonight I went to a party. It was a cancelled SXSW event my friend's client booked at the Four Seasons. The hotel wouldn't let them out of the booking. So, she decided to bring all her friends and employees out to eat the food, drink the champagne, listen to the band, and enjoy the evening out on the lawn.

It was lovely and nice to connect with friends I hadn't seen in a while, especially because two of them live in my building! I came down the elevator prepared to stroll along the trail around Lady Bird Lake to the hotel, but I ran smack into them. They were grabbing an Uber... so my lazy butt piled in. Also, it would be odd to wave them off and walk when the whole reason to get together was to... get together.

At one point in the evening, between my second and third plate of pulled pork, a lovely gentleman named Ken came over. Allison, our host for the evening, introduced all of us around the little cocktail table. In addition to Allison, CEO of Continuum Interactive, was Steph, a facial plastic surgeon, and Alicia, in operations for Maserati. When Allison introduced me, she said, "Julie does Army shit." It's always fun to hear how you're perceived; seriously, I think that was my biggest laugh of the night.

Ken asked if I knew Army Futures Command, and I explained that I was running their contract strategic communications team before starting my own company and he then said, "Oh so you know Mike!" Mike... Mike... lots of Mikes in a male-dominated group of five hundred. He meant Mike Murray, the four-star general... Cool. Ken started telling me about the first time he met Mike, and I'll save you the tale because, as we just discussed, boundaries. Just know they're buddies, k?

K.

Ken says he is a venture capitalist who does seed funding and runs a family fund, you know, doing all of those financial things. I'd recently googled the term, so I was MBA-level ready for this conversation. I told him a bit about my company and my clients. We talked about how I love what I do, I'm excited every day, and I'm much more effective on this side than I was on the inside of the bureaucracy. Then, I play the house in the poker tournament and show him a photo I got before I was NDA'd (it's open source, don't freak out).

The man doesn't blink before saying, "Send me that."

Ha!

"Nope, but I'll have coffee with you and tell you all about it." You may be wondering why I'd say that when I'm under NDA. The thing about being under an NDA is you know things about the companies that you're working with. In this case, I knew they were hunting funding like Oklahomans hunt elk.

Maybe now is a good time for all of us to talk about NDAs versus classified information. Obviously, they're not the same thing, but sometimes the information I learn when I'm read in by a client should be classified, and it's terrifying. Remember when Merlin read me in on his product? This was the story set in the Delta Lounge at LAX. I know, I'm just lounge hopping around the Western Hemisphere for fun… and I love it.

Where was I? Oh, Merlin. And Ken. At 1:44 a.m, when my darling baby woke me, I'd missed five messages in a newly created group text with Ken and my dear friend Gregory. You see, while Ken and I were chatting away, Gregory came by, and I introduced him. Gregory is one of my trusted advisors. Actually, I can't think of anyone else on that list right now. Those two hit it off, especially when Gregory explained his previous work at NASA and how he cofounded a space company. Haven't we all, Gregory?

I wonder how I'll handle Ken's request for the photo. This is the first time I've been on this side of an NDA. It might be the first time I've been on any side, actually. Sure, I signed security clearance paperwork with our dear Uncle Sam and the friendly landowner's association commonly referred to as NATO. Clearance is sacred. People die when that trust is broken. People sue when an NDA is broken. The difference is absurd.

CHAPTER 20

HELL YES YOU CAN

———

It's not because things are difficult that we dare not venture.
It's because we dare not venture that they are difficult.

—SENECA

It's March 20, 2020, a Friday night, at about 8:45 p.m. I finally decide to turn off the streaming, silence my phone, and look at the impact of COVID-19 on my baby.

Remember when it seemed like this entire book was working up to a climax of events in June? January was the building phase. February things were starting to solidify. March was going to be my launch pad. Every indication pointed to April and May continuing the trend, then we'd arrive safely at June. I hadn't counted my chickens, but I had a pretty good idea how big the coop was going to be.

And now I have to admit—I have to—this year is not going to happen the way I thought it would. I had three big events in June. FUTURES (AUSA's first Austin conference), Conceal::Reveal's first show and tell, and my first book (desperately in need of a name) would go to the editors on June 22. Three firsts! It was perfect.

[wink]

I'd told my editor, my friends, my clients… that together, FUTURES and Conceal::Reveal would establish DEFIANT. Now I need to figure out what I meant by that phrase. I need to define what "establish" means, and then I can figure out how the hell I'm going to get there without FUTURES and Conceal::Reveal.

First, I know I'm tired of feeling quarantined, caught by the feeling I've been watching a broken window crash to the ground. My mother uses this metaphor. She says sometimes the window you're looking through breaks, and the urge to rush in and put the pieces back together is irresistible. Then she cautions that you will get cut. The hardest part in these moments is waiting for all the pieces to fall. Only then can you assess and figure out what's next. I think about that whenever I have a breakup or transition.

Well, I've been waiting through five days of lockdown following all the talk and speculation of COVID-19 that filled the weeks before. I feel like I'm no clearer than I was on Monday, but I refuse to be a spectator any longer. I'm done watching the pieces fall.

So, what the fuck am I going to do now? I'm going to step outside myself and try on a different perspective.

If I lived in the building across from mine and was creepy enough to watch me through a telescope, what would I see?

I'd see a woman in half-jammies, no bra, but with clean hair and makeup. So, at some point today she gave it a shot. She went for a long walk around the lake, did a HIIT routine with a lot of squats, and managed to get some time on her yoga mat with her favorite instructor on a video. She went to Trader Joe's and put a flank steak in the crock pot. She ate cauliflower rice and asparagus, and for dinner she roasted broccolini to accompany the beef. She's adulting pretty hard right now.

Socially, she has bounced from phone calls to FaceTimes. She's good. Mentally, she has flipped a few pages in a book. She listens to audible and podcasts. She's good. Emotionally she seems stable. She laughs and smiles. Spiritually, she is connecting to her yoga mat, which means she's doing alright.

Good check in, minus the broken glass that is COVID on the floor.

* * *

When I was in Sao Paulo a few months ago, I met with Carmen, a spiritual coach. This was my first spiritual coach session. I'm an executive leadership coach by iPEC training, and I wholeheartedly believe in having a coach. I wish I'd kept up my weekly coaching calls with Hannah, but we fell into a busy life rhythm, and I lost that outside accountability. Hannah was my peer coach during training, and I was Samantha's. I love these women.

Samantha and I had a long FaceTime on Thursday. Samantha puts the "woo" in "woo-woo" and she believes in a connection to a spiritual level. I'm willing to dip my toe in Samantha's woo-woo world, because it seems to be a pretty happy place. I'm a tourist through meditation and yoga. Like *Eat, Pray, Love*, but I've just entered the "pray" phase.

I told her about my session with Carmen in Sao Paulo. Samantha's input was that we have a higher self—the person I refer to as my ideal self—and they are out there in a parallel life living the life we want.

I believe there is an ideal life for me because that would be awesome. I want ideal, doesn't everyone?

I can close my eyes and "see" this ideal. The first time I did this I was listening to a book, *Primal Leadership,* on a walk in Old Town, Alexandria. It was part of graduate school, at the very un-woo-woo Jesuit Georgetown University. The purpose of this chapter in the book, and the exercise the author put us through, was to see our ideal selves in fifteen years.

I saw it so clearly and quickly that it stopped me in my tracks. I was nearly home, at the front door, actually. I stopped and listened, then I walked inside and listened again. I stood there with my runners on not seeing anything in front of me until I realized I was standing in front of my "check your teeth before you leave" mirror. I smiled at my reflection. Moment complete.

So, what did I "see" in that future self? It was bright. I was in an old building with lots of light. People were working around me, and I was standing in the middle facing the huge windows of this historic space. I'm pretty sure I was in Arles, France, but the location is best described as "anywhere," as long as I was surrounded by light and productivity. If you could see the space I am typing this in right now, you'd laugh. It's bright, and I'm productive as fuck.

I have no children, but I was surrounded by love. Maybe I had a dog. I'm not sure. I knew I woke up to the sound of birds, and I walked to work each day. It felt like I didn't have a car, but maybe I had a light yellow Vespa I rode to work in my Italian heels. Yeah, my ideal self would totally do that. [wink]

The woman I had become was in charge of whatever enterprise surrounded her. She was successful. Her world was clean, uncluttered, and focused.

Hmm… it's nice to remember that vision of my ideal self because it has evolved, but not much. When I told the spiritual coach in Sao Paulo about it, I told her all of those things. I told Samantha, too. Samantha told me only that version of me knows the path from here to there. She's the only one who has done it, so, of course, she's the only one who can guide me.

A guide sounds nice right now...

* * *

Woo-woo complete, and back to business.

Guidance. I'll take two, please! I am five days into self-imposed quarantine, and I'd love it if someone could tell me how to get from now to that picture of success (in all aspects of my life). Woo-woo aside, I may as well do the exercise of working backwards from that picture to the half-jammied version of myself on the couch right now.

Here goes... this is me trusting that I can get to success. I know where I want to be. I know my purpose. I know my business's purpose, and that hasn't changed—not one bit! I have to let go of the way I thought I would achieve it, otherwise I'll just be holding bits of broken glass so tightly in my fists that I'll get cut. I thought June was it. It's not, and that's okay. It's better than okay. [wink] It's good, and it's great! I don't need FUTURES, and I don't need Conceal::Reveal. Although, I really like the name and I bought the .com...

Focus Jules. What does the warfighter need right now for this moment during COVID-19? Do they need anything new? I mean, let's look at some options. Maybe they have what they need? What about martial law? At that point we'd have soldiers on the streets, and shit would get weird. They would need to be safe, and they would need their own physical security. Maybe this is my pivot to somewhere in there. Maybe this is my pivot to biotech. Biotech security? A lot of money is flying into biotech right now. Maybe I should take everything I learned as a kid, with a microbiologist for a mother, and go that direction.

Maybe the military will double down on the idea of H2F (Holistic Health and Fitness). I wonder. I wonder if there's something there...

Is the moment I double down on soldier readiness the moment I'm leaning against my cold granite kitchen counter, half-jammied, a claw clip in my hair, pants with four holes in the crotch that should never go outside? ...is this what the moment looks like?

Maybe.

But no, it's not. My purpose and the mission of my company is not to sustain the concept of soldier readiness. It's modernization, motherfuckers. Readiness is a trap. It's stagnant. It's the trap we've been in for decades, and I don't want to be stagnant.

* * *

Last night felt good. I didn't get any answers, but I was open to the idea of "maybe." What could the future of DEFIANT look like without the bookend of June to mark the finale of a few initiatives?

That exercise was real and one a lot of small business owners can relate to right now. It's honest. It's also bullshit.

Why? Because those were pieces in my path that I'd lined up. FUTURES, Conceal::Reveal, and the climax of this book. Boom, boom, and... boom. They didn't matter to DEFIANT until I decided they did.

They were just things on the calendar. The last few months have been such a sprint that it's a welcome change to be able to see where I am and refocus. First, I've come pretty far in a few months. I went from little miss Thomas the Tank engine "I think I canning" all over the map to "holy shit when am I going to jail?" It was a lot all at once.

...and I miss it. Oh, how I miss it!!! It's not just that I've run out of on-demand television to watch on Netflix, Amazon Prime, and Hulu with Showtime. It's that I was expanding at such a pace that I couldn't keep up. It was amazing. Sure, at one point I was pretty freaked out that I was almost an international arms dealer. You and I know if I could have taken one more step in that direction, I would have.

I spent a couple hours today flipping through grants.gov and reminiscing about my longtime desire to be a *National Geographic* explorer. So, I want to own an empire, moonlight as a *NatGeo* explorer, daylight as an arms dealer, and weekend alone on a sunny yacht. The things I've seen since I started this company opened me up to the possibility that any, or all, of those can happen. For example, the Borg that Merlin built is on ice right now. It can fly and collect data; data that can be analyzed. So, why don't I rub a couple of my brain cells together and hatch a truly batshit-crazy plan to rule the world?

What I need to do now is to convince Merlin to let me borrow one of his precious multi-million-dollar prototypes and use it to do something useful—like scan the ground in Poland for unexploded land mines. Yeah, that's still a thing that needs to be done. Shocking, right?

The State Department has an open solicitation out for companies to bid on the work of finding and removing those land mines. I'm not suggesting in the middle of a pandemic we go out and hunt mines. I'm suggesting we fly a pretty little

UFO over fields to test if we can detect them. Then we can send robots in to pop the tops off those buggers.

What's the harm in that? Depends on who you're asking. First, I doubt the Poles want a UFO in the sky scaring their people in the middle of a global pandemic. Do you know what we don't need right now? Aliens! Now would be a very inconvenient time for their arrival on Earth. Also, the Poles probably don't want a UFO stamped with "Made in the USA" flying in their airspace at all. Even if we could convince the State Department to give us funding to test the technology, they'd need to spend some political capital to get the Poles to agree.

But... it's a damn good idea. No aliens, and no one gets close to any bombs. It's a win-win!

Growing up, especially in my teen years, whenever my mother would leave the house she'd say, "No parties. No boys." Who knew she'd have a daughter who says, "No aliens. No bombs."

[sigh]

Maybe it's a good thing I don't have children.

I saw something on the *NatGeo* page about surveying historical sites, but I dismissed it at first. What if I flip this equation and instead of running guns, (legally) I use my powers for good? What if I use innovation to deconstruct weapons or to use their capabilities in a softer, sweeter way? I could do that. I could use UFOs to monitor erosion of historically/culturally/architecturally significant sites. Hell, I did work alongside the Office of Cultural Heritage at the State Department when I was a contractor years ago. They're the ones who sent me to historical sites in Peru and Jordan where I posed for the photos that give my online dating profiles that special something. [wink]

What the hell? I'll give it a shot.

8:52 p.m. Text

Me: Merlin, I'm considering a NatGeo grant, and I need to know if I can borrow a Lynx to scan archeological sites

Thirty-six minutes later...

Merlin: Hell yes you can

Then, he sends me a fourteen-page document with details on the capabilities of the cameras he'd recommend for this. Um... okay.

PART 5

PIVOT

CHAPTER 21

74 MINUTES

———

Give a girl the right shoes, and she can conquer the world.
—MARILYN MONROE

April 22, 2020

I thought I did all the work. I thought I watched all the pieces fall. When COVID started, I had to let go of everything that DEFIANT was doing for June. I thought I let it all go, but I forgot about one piece.

It's 2:15 p.m. today when AUSA calls.

"I'm sure it's no surprise to you that AUSA's June event, FUTURES, is canceled. So, I want you to hear it from me and talk to you about the path forward." she begins.

Nope. Not a surprise, but I'm disappointed. There will be a gap because people need to network, and this is a missed opportunity. The conversation didn't end there, though.

"...if you wouldn't mind billing us for any services that you have debts incurred and all the time that you took at AUSA offices and such... return any funds that we haven't used and we'll keep it clean on the books."

Oh fuck. What? By the end of the call I am bursting with the need to burst. So, they weren't going to roll anything into the big annual conference in October. They were done with all things FUTURES-related this year. That means I'm not going to get the rest of the money. The kicker? They want any money back that had not been accounted for, allocated, or spent, returned.

Logistically, how am I supposed to do that? We agreed on a flat rate to avoid doing hourly work, and now I'm stuck. I don't know how to do this. I'm David, and they're Goliath's whole family.

I cashed that check, and I was depending on it.

Oh great, I have another call at 4:00 p.m. I have less than an hour and a half to lose my shit, and have my mobster buddha, Tony, duct-tape me back together.

I have seventy-four minutes. I feel like the floor of my high-rise apartment had suddenly disappeared under my chair. By the time I look up from crying at my desk, I realize I'd already lost eight of those precious seventy-four minutes. Finally, I zombie walk to the bedroom and plop down on my bed facing the ceiling. I land slightly askew, but I don't stay that way for long. Can't have a turning point and be—literally—off center! Just because I feel like my foundation is disappearing doesn't mean I'm going to crumble with it.

Back to the business at hand. Tears flowing into my ears—so gross, seriously. Who put tear ducts in line with ear canals? It's stupid.

What do I do now?

After I met the spiritual coach in Sao Paulo, I picked up a book on manifesting at a local yoga studio there. I read it on the plane. It was short, and I followed along and wrote my intentions down. Eventually, I downloaded the app and recorded them. These are the things I want for my life and my business—the deep stuff, the stuff I don't tell people because I think they might judge me for wanting to have scrambled eggs for breakfast on my yacht.

Don't laugh! I swear, this would bring me love and joy. I imagine it's like hotel breakfast but… brighter, sunnier, more blue, and maybe a little breezy. I don't know. I've never been on a yacht.

I opened the app, hit play, set it to repeat, and laid the phone on my chest.

More tears. Ten minutes… twenty minutes… thirty minutes… pass.

I've heard these words how many times? I wrote them, I recorded them, and I've listened to them for six weeks. I know them. The difference this time is how naked I feel hearing my own voice. I'm exposed to everything now. There is no shell. No designer label suit of armor I can project success from. No big organization that believes in me. I am one hundred percent out here on my own.

Again.

Is this how failure feels? Nothing between me and smacking into the ground below. I feel naked. Ugh. I don't want to splat feeling naked.

Did I fail? Is this it?

I know every breath and inflection in the recording. It's only eighty-three seconds. I close my eyes and zone in and out.

"My business grows stronger and more global every day, and I am so very grateful for the adventure… how it spreads peace and security, light and love."

My eyes flew open. My next call! A conversation with a group of people who were retooling their production facility to make emergency ventilators. Global adventure spreading peace and security calling for a Ms. Willis. Is there a Ms. Willis on the line?

Armor. I need armor. Does any of my good stuff even fit anymore? Stupid COVID-19. I grab six black dresses and toss them on the bed. One after another I try them on looking for something substantive. I can't go into this call feeling naked.

One of them works. It's snug. I wouldn't wear it outside, but it's tight enough to remind me I'm not naked. It'll have to do. I open my shoe cabinet and pull out my most badass heels. Okay, wow, these are remarkably uncomfortable after not wearing heels for five weeks. Heels are done. I need lipstick. This is as close as we're going to find to armor in this condo. I apply the Christian Dior red holding court on top of my shoe cabinet. Yep, it really brings out the puffiness in my eyes.

With a mix of disdain for the blue velvet office chair that just witnessed my cryfest and the faux grace of a woman wearing a black dress, four-inch heels, and Christian Dior red lipstick, I dial in to the conference line.

"It sounds like we have a couple other people joining in," I hear.

"This is Julie."

"Julie, how are you?"

"Good…," I mean, maybe.

CHAPTER 22

CONFERENCE TABLE

——

Our life is what our thoughts make it.

—MARCUS AURELIUS

Being an entrepreneur was a lot more fun when it came with travel. Now that my radius is confined to how far I can walk, it's less fun. It's not any less stressful, and the stakes haven't changed. I still eat what I kill, and it doesn't look like killing season out there.

It is, though. It has to be. It always will be. There is no off-season in this "sport." Right now, baseball is trying to figure out how to play during COVID-19. I get it. I want to play, too!

My dear, dear woo-woo-coach friend Samantha, and fellow entrepreneur, left me a video message on the Marco Polo app crying on Thursday. She was responding to the Polo I'd left for her the day before. I was crying in that one. Startup CEO life is a roller coaster with nothing to hold you in when it goes upside down. The scenery is always changing, and you never know what's behind the next curve, or what's ahead.

We agreed to meet for a coffee walk the next morning. I wake up to my alarm at 7:20 a.m. and see a text from Samantha asking if we could bump our start time from 8:00 a.m. to 8:15 a.m. Um… yeah.

I snooze the alarm.

I don't get my butt out of bed until 8:00 a.m. I send her a quick note at 8:10 a.m. as I brush my teeth. "U left yet?"

Three minutes later I get the reply. "I'm here."

Damn it! I'm not dressed. I pull it together and head out to get my Samantha fix. Oh, and my caffeine fix because I'm clearly in need today.

Samantha is special. She is the furthest thing from the defense industry in my life. She believes in energy healing, crystals, tarot, astrology, past lives, angels, parallel universes… all of it. She once told me our souls made a pact to check in on each other during this life. I could overthink that, but it's probably better that I don't spend a lot of time contemplating if/how souls make plans to hang out on Earth. I'm just grateful she's in my world. Spending time with Samantha feels like a vacation from the finite mindset of the military. Samantha was in my cohort in 2019 at the iPEC coaching program. She's a life coach now, among many other things, but when I met her, she had just moved to Austin, too.

During the coaching program, I was her peer coach, so I know a lot about Samantha. As her coach, I held the space for her to process the move, find clarity in her business, launch it, and keep it on the path to success. I had a VIP ticket to her thoughts and emotions. I love this woman.

All the woo-woo and fluffy stuff doesn't shield her from being human. She struggles with all the same parts of being an entrepreneur that everyone else does. She launched her podcast on December 30, 2019... two days before I started DEFIANT. We're sisters in startup life.

We agree to walk to Jo's, on Second Street, and putz around.

"Alright girl. What happened on Wednesday?" She kicks off our walk by kicking it over to me.

"So..." I don't know where to begin. "AUSA called at like 2:15 p.m. to tell me they were fully cancelling the June event and they would not be rolling my contract into the annual meeting in October. Their leadership wanted to clean the books and I was told to send back the money I hadn't earned."

"How much is that?"

"I don't have a clue!"

We pass the beautiful architecture of downtown Austin and cross the old railroad track bridge. "I rode my bike over this yesterday," Samantha says. "It's so beautiful!" It is. Austin is gorgeous in spring. It's green and happy. The polished high-rise windows of Google and Proper, the newest posh hotel, reflect all the blue and wispy clouds in the sky.

"What is this?" Samantha asks.

"This is Proper. It's lovely. Andrew and I had dinner in there once, and I've had brunch a couple times out here on the patio."

"Was dinner good?"

"I liked it." We smile at each other and laugh. Six weeks or so have passed since Andrew and I broke up, so nobody is going to waste calories analyzing and creating action plans to improve the next date (women do this all day long, folks). The truth is he had branzino, his favorite fish, and it came whole. I watched with detached amusement as he picked every bone out. I have no idea what I had.

Samantha and I agree to have brunch there someday when things reopen. It's an easy promise to make. I don't spoil the moment by pointing out it was stupid expensive. It doesn't matter when things are closed.

"Okay," I go back to our topic and start my rant again. "So AUSA and I agreed to do a flat rate for a reason, right? Now they want me to assign hours to things and a rate—both of which we never discussed. I had a rate in one of the early proposals, but in the two-hour call that followed when I was in Vegas, they asked for a flat rate. I have no idea what to do with that. Do I charge them for those hours? Do I charge them at that hourly rate? When do I start the clock? Does it start when I was first told they would sign with me on February 7 after I'd spent three days playing tour guide with them in Austin? Or does it start when they finally signed the contract on March 11?"

I finally run out of steam as we get to Jo's. "I have no fucking clue," is my finale. Rant complete. Neither of us know how to proceed so it just ends, and we order coffee.

* * *

"Alright, so what is happening with you?" I ask as we head South to the trail. I already know from her teary-eyed Polo that she's doubting herself and the business. It's complicated by COVID-19, of course, but it's deeper than that.

"Girl, I just don't know what I'm doing. It makes sense for a minute, but then I just don't know. I'm not making any money. I don't qualify for the PPP or the stimulus because I didn't have taxes last year. All the gigs I had for conferences have been postponed until 2021! Not later this year; totally gone until next year. I can't even make money doing that now. I have no coaching clients right now and my podcast is just out there."

Instead of walking the trail we divert to a shady bench. Sitting as far from each other as we can, in case any six-foot public shaming breaks out, we settle in. "Where is the Samantha from last Friday? She was setting up her Patreon account and expanding in every direction!"

"Oh my god," she sighs. Startup founders will identify with this moment, and the rest of you might be wondering how she can transition from vision and action to crying on a park bench so quickly. Let me assure you, a week is a long time to wait for the pendulum to swing. I can go from feeling like a complete badass to "holy shit I'm going to be broke" in as long as it takes to have that thought. If I've learned anything this year, it's that the power to dismiss the negative thoughts and return to a general state of badassery is the only thing that will make or break my startup. It's not about money. A founder with a million dollars in the bank will bankrupt themselves if they can't command their own badassery.

This is where being Samantha's coach comes in handy. She already knows the question I'm going to ask next, and that's why we're together on a park bench that kind of smells like pee. If she intended to stay in "holy shit I'm going to be broke" she would not have left me that Polo. She would have kept the thought to herself and made it a nice little home where it could colonize and build a suburb.

"What has changed since I saw you last Friday?" I ask.

Samantha takes a sharp inhale and holds it. "I talked to my brother." AHA! She exhales just as sharply. "He offered to invest in my company. I should be excited that he'd do that.

He's so smart. My dad was an entrepreneur, my brothers are in business... they are all super successful."

"Ok, so why is that not a good thing?"

"It's just..." she collects all the "justs" in her head and prioritizes. "He thinks I should be doing YouTube and I get it, but he has no idea how hard it is to do everything I'm doing already. I'm creating the content. I'm the one finding the people to interview. I'm the one coordinating everything. I'm writing the summary. I'm posting to social media. I'm doing the newsletter. I'm doing all of it already. I can't add YouTube, too!"

Tears fall.

"Samantha," I put my coach hat down and put on my friend hat, "do you have any idea how big the conference room is in your head? Imagine if you had to hire all the people who you already have to be—just enough—to have come this far? This town is full of conference room tables, and it would take a building worth of people just to pull off what you're already doing. You've got legal, and accounting and... all of it. Plus, you're an influencer so you have to have the lighting people and the makeup people and the stylists and the PR..."

This hits home. She's still crying, but now she's validated. We're sitting in front of Silicon Labs with our backs to the building. It's a huge company that needs all of those people. An entrepreneur has to be each of them to the level they know they need them, but they can't be them. It's madness. The impossibility of being your own lawyer, accountant, banker, IT team, etc. You could spend your whole life learning how to be the people you need because you know you can't afford to hire them. Figuring out how to be okay with that and stay in a general state of badassery is a lesson taught by the school of hard knocks. I don't care what the MBA program websites say. If you don't have the awareness and ability to manage how you talk to yourself, don't become an entrepreneur.

"I'm going to get in the weeds with you because… I already am. I've spent a lot of time lately thinking about this conference table. Somehow, I have to accept how limited I am and keep my unlimited vision alive. It sure was easier when I was spinning my cute little carryon into the posh little airport lounges," we laugh.

"Samantha," I ask with a little trepidation, "is this the moment when we agree to work together?"

It was not an eloquent ask. I'm sure we've both thought about it, but I'm so focused on the military stuff and she's the mayor of woo-woo. Sure, I've thought a lot about the roles I'm able to fill at my own conference table lately, but I've also missed the feeling that comes from doing the real work. I miss being able to play and create. I'd already become accustomed to the aloneness of my business, but without the client interaction, I'm in a closed feedback loop. I crave being with someone and discussing my ideas and products.

"Uh yeah. I mean, what does that look like?"

"Shrug emoji? Look, if you give me your logins I'll poke around and let you know what I see. My brain is hungry to work, you'd be doing me a favor." Normally I don't follow the ask with a verbal emoji reference, nor do I ask for their passwords so I can poke around in their accounts. I can't imagine a situation where I've asked anyone for that, outside of a signed contract stating I'll need access in order to pull analytics.

"Sure. Do whatever you want."

Oh, how I love to hear that! Now I have a playground in the woo-woo world where no one has heard of all the norms and customs I usually play by. How fun!

* * *

I keep thinking about building a conference room and sitting at my conference table. A week later, I check my phone after saying "namaste" to my favorite yoga teacher, JJ, on my iPad. It is 10:36 a.m. on Thursday, and I have a text from my coach, Hannah. We had a session on the calendar at 1:00 p.m., and I am really hoping she isn't cancelling. She has a day job—with a boss and everything—so it's possible.

It turns out, Hannah just needed to talk. It's hard to have a weekly coaching session that acknowledges how things are going for her, too. I am so touched she turned to me. I feel like I dump on her for fifty-eight minutes of our weekly hour together. She was my peer coach in training, just like I was Samantha's.

Hannah and her husband plan to move to Colorado "someday." All of their family is in the Austin area, and with a three-year-old, it's hard to leave. There's something calling both of them to Colorado, more specifically the Denver metro area. I was there last year on a little Spirit Airlines adventure. It was my first time, and I came back to Austin calling it "flat Denver."

I share the piece about Hannah and Colorado with all of you because it comes up in my session later that day and surprises both of us. We spend the entire hour talking about how I wish I could go around a conference table in my head and ask all of the roles and responsibilities in there—by job title—what they're working on and what they will get done by 5:00 p.m. on Friday. The Friday at five thing comes straight out of the Brendon Burchard podcast I sometimes listen to on my walks around the lake. Brendon is a *lot*. I have to be in the mood for him.

I can only take so much motivational speaking and productivity tools in the middle of COVID-19. I know you know what I mean. Lately, I've been in the mood, and I've realized I'm slipping. When the stay-at-home order came down, I did like all the other non-essential people and stayed at home. I used the "get over Andrew plan" I'd written on the plane back from D.C. on March 5 to keep me organized. It mainly consisted of kicking ass in every area of my life—because that's what you do when you want the other person to feel shitty the next time they see you or ask how you're doing. "I'm great!"

Do me a favor and read that again with the Tony the Tiger voice. "I'm grrrreat!" What did I have to lose if I repurposed the "get over Andrew plan?" Nothing. Just more awesomeness. So, I went hour by hour from the moment my alarm went off to the moment I turned off the bedside lamp. I had time built in for three focus areas: body, brain, and business.

Six weeks into staying at home, I had maintained momentum on body and brain, but business was slipping. However, I did a lot of writing and kept a positive attitude. I didn't lose any sleep over the contract I lost for FUTURES. I carried on. I'm grateful and not surprised. "Head down, plow through" is my racehorse gear. I can get a lot done on that gear, with my blinders on, but I will burn out.

If I had ever owned a horse, I would give you a metaphor; but I never have, and I think we're both better off without one. Hannah probably has. I bet it's a thing they check when you move to Colorado. I know, you're waiting for me to close the loop on that. Here it goes: we spent an entire hourlong session building my conference room. In my head. If I'd done it alone, I might be a little concerned to have an imaginary conference table with imaginary people that I roleplay in order to act out a business meeting like a grown up.

"Hi, I'm Barbie and this is Ken." I'm kidding. Remember the exercise I did in graduate school on my ideal self? I can still see Ideal Julie. She pops right back up from the first time I did that exercise. The office is bright and white with a huge cathedral window. On the left is a painted-over brick wall. There are desks around. Whenever I visualize this space, I'm in the middle of the room facing the window. There seems to be an area to have a conference room somewhere to the right, but I'd have to build a hallway and other things—too much work.

I know I want light. And greenery. "Ooh! It's a rooftop garden!" I exclaim.

In the positive voice of a mother of a three-year-old, Hannah says, "Okay!"

"It's… the garden isn't all the way around. There has to be a door. But yeah. It's on the roof, and it's surrounded by glass." I start to sketch it out on my notepad. I've got a big-long rectangle table in a big rectangle room—one seat at the top and one at the bottom by the door.

"Espresso bar!" It's so obvious, yet I nearly left it out.

"Trees… got to make sure they're outside… okay." I've now sketched a pathetic tree the only way I learned how when I was five. Someone call the permitting office because this is as good as any CAD drawing.

It came to a screeching halt. "Uh oh," I say.

"Uh oh, what?"

"I don't know how many chairs. Do I have to decide now?"

I am conscious of the fact Hannah is patiently holding the space for a grown ass woman to build a conference room in the sky. This never escapes either of us.

Yet, Hannah answers. "You can always move the chairs."

I take a quick aha breath, "You're right! But let me think… I need people now."

"Ok, who do you need now?"

"I need legal. I need accounting. No, I need a CFO. Wait, do I want that level at the table? No. I want doers. What is that title?"

Hannah smiles because she is an accountant and works for a CFO. "You want a controller."

"Ooh fancy. Yes. I'll take one of those."

Eventually I seat myself at the bottom of the page, closest to the espresso bar. I called dibs. At the far end of the table is my COO. I seat legal, the controller, client services, HR, IT, and marketing. Everyone is assembled. It's beautiful. It's simple. It's open.

It hits me.

I've been here before. It's the fucking rooftop espresso bar at the Contemporary Museum of Modern Art in downtown Denver. My ideal self has daily standup meetings in the rooftop garden of the museum. I grab my phone and am so excited I can't search my photos to show Hannah. I pull up the location in Denver and there is a photo in Google.

Colorado, man. Colorado.

If you thought this story ended there, you were being a little optimistic. Once I let Hannah go back to her real job, I pinged Kyle on WhatsApp. "Hi." The man stood me up last weekend for a phone call so this was as nice as I was willing to be. I am still riding the high of the coaching call and feeling generous.

Ten minutes later, a video call comes through from him. I tell him the story I just told you about building my conference room. He sent me a calendar invite for next Thursday at 3:00 p.m. to check in with me and my "team." It's nice to have a sanity check. If Kyle is willing to entertain this, it's possible I haven't gone COVID-crazy.

That's what I thought. Then, Kyle doubles down on the conference room and challenges me to hire two interns to fill two of those positions for the summer.

"For some of these graduates, the jobs they lined up have disappeared," he says. He's making sense. "By next week, choose two of those chairs and decide on the roles and responsibilities of the positions they'll fill. I will send you a calendar invite for a progress report next week."

"Challenge accepted." A little fear creeps in as it dawns on me that this man is going to make a real CEO out of me.

CHAPTER 23

SBA FAST PROGRAM

———

One of the things I learned the hard way was that it doesn't pay to get discouraged. Keeping busy and making optimism a way of life can restore your faith in yourself.

—LUCILLE BALL

Surprise! Writing a book involves a lot of writing.

I couldn't be more grateful. Am I enjoying it? A little. It's nice to get the thoughts out of my head. I'm processing how COVID-19 has changed our lives... one word at a time.

I'm also processing how my idea of DEFIANT is changing. I feel like I'm walking in the dark, and I'm lost. It doesn't help that I keep bumping into new problems.

I'll take a few steps in a row and get some momentum going, only to misjudge the next step and smack into something rigid. I want to crawl under my dining room table and hide.

While writing this book, the U.S. has gone from abundance to social distancing. We've changed in a short period of time, and the future "normal" is beyond anything any of us can see right now. We simply don't know where the obstacles are anymore. The distance between today and the next game changing innovation is hard to see, too. However, we know it's coming.

I was flying around meeting those game-changers just a month or two ago. I've seen the tech, and I know it'll be here before we know it. (Probably because it'll quietly transfer hands.) Presumably, many of that tech will follow the SBIR contracting path. In fact, a lot of the vaccine research money is going through the SBIR funnel.

My Google calendar is full of webinars on SBIRs right now. I wake up on Friday and check my calendar, from bed— just looking for an excuse to not get up and get moving. Finding no excuses, besides a webinar this afternoon from the SBA itself, I get up and out on the trail.

I don't remember signing up for this one, and I can't find any related emails. It's like a gift from the angels—haha, said no Zoom attendee ever.

It's a typical Friday in COVID-19-land. I see the purple meeting on my calendar for Friday at 5:00 p.m. to go through my conference table and see how all the functions of DEFI-ANT fared. There is no significance in the color. I wanted it to pop! Friday at five is sacred. It's the "what did you do this week for the business" deadline. I blow by it every time!

Oh, I'm the worst CEO.

Thankfully, I have other talents, like a willingness to sit through brutally boring webinars on dry topics. So far this week, I've had the equivalent of three workdays worth. I dialed into one of them during my morning walk on the trail. I did a full lower body workout during another one. I keep seeing the same problem in each one. To submit a strong proposal, you need an MOU or Letter of Support. No one seems to know how to get those without hiring a consultant, or a member of the O-6 Rolodex Mafia. This is madness. No wonder companies give up on federal R&D.

Dear Warfighter,

Hey, how are things?

Quick update from here. We can't afford to pay to get connected to an MOU signatory. So, our SBIR proposal is not going to happen.

We sure hope someone else has the money or the relationships, and the same capability. Otherwise, you're fucked.

Love,

Defense Innovators

It's SBA webinar time! When there is $125K on the line, suddenly I'm paying attention. I even prep and ask questions. Amazing.

I learned that the SBA awards twenty-four grants across the U.S. for outreach and engagement of SBIR and small business technology transfer (STTR) per year. Only one grant can be awarded per state, and the governor's office can only endorse one. There are twenty-four awards and fifty states. It doesn't add up for me either, but I don't have anything to lose.

I think a marketing funnel, like the type Brendon Burchard uses to spread his message, could help reach and educate small businesses and drive interest in pursuing SBIRs. Now I need to figure out what that looks like practically and try to sell it to the state of Texas. No big deal. I need to be the Brendon Burchard of R&D. That should take a day or two, right?

* * *

Back in March, when we all went home and put our jammies on for a couple weeks, I filled out a grant application for small businesses. It was for five thousand dollars from Hello Alice. I did not get the money, but I did get a lot of emails.

Months later, in the fog of COVID-19 time, I caught a LinkedIn post from the Founder Institute advertising an upcoming interview between their CEO and the CEO of Hello Alice. What did I have to lose? It's not like I can't tune in for a couple minutes, and, if I tune out, I can walk away. Well, she made some good points about entrepreneurship. I have no idea what they are now, but she impressed me, so I start opening the emails that didn't start with, "Here's Five Thousand Dollars!"

One of those emails invites me to a two-week course on reopening my business with resilience. Resilience sounds nice. I've been open, from my apartment, this whole time but not exactly resilient about it. I have plenty of toilet paper and zero resilience right now.

I sign up, and the next thing I did was to ignore the first email on Monday. I'm just being honest here. I feel low. I don't have the energy to think positively about my future. Thankfully, I wake up on Tuesday with a little pep in my step.

Today, Wednesday, when I wake up and pull open the blackout curtains, my sliding glass doors are covered in pink and purple writing. I completely forgot I did that yesterday. It took three hours to complete step one from Monday's email, but I did it. There's no way I could have done it on Monday because there is a very frank moment when they ask you to choose how you're going to proceed: fold, tweak, or pivot. They use nicer terms than those, but that's a real deal kind of moment. Me and the laptop... alone together... choosing to tweak.

I've been trying to pivot for weeks, and it feels more like spinning. Doing the work yesterday helped me get clarity around my goals, what success looks like, how to divvy up my time and energy, and where I'm heading. Sure, my evening devolved into making a list on Airbnb titled "Next" with thirty-plus homes I intend to live in for six months. They're all half the price of what I'm paying now, so... I might have made two great plans in one day! Every single one is outside the United States.

Bottom line, here's what I realized: 40 percent of my time needs to be spent on the book (hi), 40 percent spent on developing my media empire, and 20 percent on existing client relationships. I do need funds now, and Brett is ready to do some "Julie sustaining" work. Yeah, Brett's back.

I need seed money to grow my media empire! I can't be Brendon Burchard next week without a little cash. I realized, while covering the sliding glass doors with my thoughts, the funnel I envision is all new media. So, I'm loosely calling DEFIANT's pivot in that direction "my media empire." Also, that sounds like the kind of pivot that could happen during COVID-19.

Imagine this: DEFIANT Communication, the company formerly providing strategic communication services to defense entrepreneurs, has emerged from the pandemic as DEFIANT Media.

Sure. That's a cute story.

* * *

On Thursday, I wrote an email to the five people I trust with this idea.

Good morning!

I'm working on a proposal for the SBA's FAST Program grant application. It is federal money, up to $125K per award, to conduct outreach and proposal assistance for SBIR/STTR grants. I want to disrupt the O-6 Rolodex Mafia that controls access to MOU signatories.

My program idea is new to the SBA/SBIR/STTR ecosystem, but it is based on best practices and emerging trends in my field (strategic communication). It offers an alternative to the capture management companies, and the retainer/commission model, through monetization of on-demand resources that startups and small businesses can afford.

I think. :) Here's the funnel:

1. *Podcast - with two-tiered monthly membership options for VIP access/perks (five to ten dollars)*

2. *Webinars - hosted on-demand (twenty dollars)*

3. *Facebook Live - group coaching included on paid membership of podcast/webinar (networking/teaming opportunity)*

4. *Online Courses - specific content for different agencies and funding cycles (at least two hundred dollars)*

I love the idea of serving the ecosystem with high fidelity content, especially at an affordable price for companies exploring SBIR/STTR options. The purpose of the FAST Program funding is to drive applications in that state, and therefore more awards, from underrepresented groups (women-owned, hubzone, etc.). I am confident that utilizing a free and fun digital platform, such as the podcast, will drive engagement and inspire people to pursue this funding. I am also confident that using a digital approach transcends state lines and is complementary to other state programs, and therefore the entire SBIR/STTR ecosystem.

Now... for the tricky part. Due to the number of SBIR/STTR awards in Texas, the FAST Program requires a one-to-one match for funds. I can use revenue projections in that calculation, but I'm going to need sponsors and partners.

I see this as a phenomenal opportunity for a system integrator (prime) to build brand awareness and their potential teaming network. However, I also see incubators/accelerators/VCs as an option. This is where I need help. If you have ideas or contacts you think may be interested, please let me know.

The grant recently opened and closes June 19.

Best,

Julie

* * *

In order to send that email, I have to commit to this funnel, with or without the FAST Program money. I can't ask someone else to put dollars on the line if I'm not willing to put my time into it.

Finally, I can see next steps instead of trying to figure out where to put my energy. I can go back to doing the actual work again! Woohoo!

CHAPTER 24

TRUTH

———

There are only two mistakes one can make along the road to truth; not going all the way, and not starting.

—BUDDHA

Email May 7 9:56 a.m.
Hi Heather!
I'd like to ask a favor. Do you think your friend Kara would be willing to jump on a call with me? I'm meeting a publisher today, and I've finished the first 20K words, so I'm starting to wonder what's next. It would be great to be able to ask those candid questions. I fully expect to pay for her time.
Best,
Julie

Email May 7 10:22 a.m.

Dear Julie—just sent Kara a huge text! And... of course I talked to her last week and raved about you!!!! I gave Kara your mobile number. Let's give her a few moments to respond.

Email May 7 10:32 a.m.

Thank you, love!

I had no idea what I was getting myself into by agreeing to write this book, that much should be obvious to you. When it began, I was bopping around talking to smart people who were making shit happen. COVID-19 put an end to that, and we need to figure out what's next.

Kara, a former publicist for *the* leading bestseller list is no longer in the industry, but she sure knew what I needed to hear today.

"Unfortunately, I can see the problem, and I know what's causing it," I said. "That controversy is what makes it compelling, otherwise it's just, 'There was a chick with an American Express card who hung out in airport lounges for a while.'"

Kara responded, "Book publishers are looking for somebody that has a proven track record of selling books. Most people now are writing books or self-publishing books to provide credibility as they go on the speaker circuit."

"Yeah, I've noticed that in a lot of the questionnaires. They ask where you want to speak and I'm like, 'I don't want to be the poster child of calling out a defense industry payola ring,' because that's not what I'm in it for."

That comment hangs out there—along with the question of WHY I am in this.

I inhale.

"I'm really just in it to add context to policy and hope that this book can move the conversation forward. I'm idealistic, can you tell?"

Kara tells me, "Self-publishing is all good and well, but the biggest challenge is still marketing the book. You may have the most powerful interesting fascinating whistleblower story out there but nobody's going to know about it."

Oh my god, that is not okay. Paying for access to MOU signatories is corrupt as fuck and we owe our warfighters better. I did not come this far to have nobody know about it. But holy cow, I really don't want to do this.

"There is definitely fear wrapped around it a little..." I trail off to exhale, "...or a lot. It's a David and Goliath type of thing, and there are quite a few Goliaths. I'm hoping to find a way through the story where it lands softly and in a way that is more palatable for the reader."

Yes. Palatable. Except I swear constantly. I really don't know what the hell I am doing.

"When you say, and I'm just going to be really direct with you..." she starts.

"Please do." I say.

"When you say 'lands softly' that means nobody sees it. That means it goes nowhere."

Shit.

"Fair enough," is all I can manage. She's right.

"Does somebody else have more credibility or have the right initials behind their name, to be the voice behind this and you can be the one backing it up?" she asks, trying to help me out here...

Nope. I don't think anybody else either has the perspective or the balls to say it.

"I don't... I don't see anyone else on my immediate radar. Which is fine, because most of them can't anyway. They're not going to step out of line, certainly not on the government side, because their careers depend on it, and in this economy, nobody's going to jeopardize that. On the industry side, they're too caught up in trying to not rock the boat that they'd never admit publicly that they're trapped, or they're making a shit ton of money off of R&D dollars. This is the same pot of money the government is using for COVID-19 vaccine research," I say shutting down the help Kara tried to offer me. It's not just the balls or perspective, it's that they lack the incentive even though... again... back to my "why:" they're dying.

Kara moves the conversation back to the tactical. "Does the program you're in offer any tips or training from a marketing standpoint?"

"The guy running the program has been saying for six or eight weeks to announce it on LinkedIn. Going into COVID-19, I really thought June was going to be the climax of my book and the projects in my business."

Then I lie.

"...which is fine." It's not fine.

"I think my answer here is no," I manage to circle back to the question she asked and not fall down the dark hole that is my original business plan. "Their advice is to build your audience and be vulnerable, which has really not been my thing. I haven't pursued doing social media because I feel like I'm telling the story in the book, not play by play on Instagram."

"If you're not doing it on Instagram, nobody's looking at picking up the book."

Will this woman please stop telling me what I need to know? Goodness gracious... the honesty is a lot.

* * *

LinkedIn Article May 10

I'm writing a book!

Did you know that means I need to engage on social media now? Well, I'm not sure I would have agreed to do this if I'd known. Professionally it makes sense, but personally—yikes!

I've decided the only way I can be vulnerable on here and Instagram is to be a total nut about it. Stay tuned, folks. It's gonna get weird.

You may have seen this post. I wrote it and left out one key piece: this was not my idea. I was sitting outside on the balcony trying to write my "hello world" post when my girlfriend, Jessica, interrupted me asking if I wanted coffee. Don't I always?

We traipse down the street to Nate's and have a great chit chat. Just like Kara, Jessica had no trouble calling me out on my shit. Is it stuck in my hair or something? I don't usually get so much feedback on my crap.

Over a ridiculously expensive can of CBD-infused sparkling water, I tell Jessica everything: my insecurities, my desire to share the book with people I don't know and not the people I do... and that I have got to find a way to show up on social media. I told her I don't want my ex-boyfriends to find me on social media. (Two already have, and I am up to fifty-four followers—seriously?)

It's on that outdoor stool in downtown Austin that Jessica suggests I just own how reluctant I am.

"Share the stories from the book and make sure your face is on them. People click on photos with faces."

"How the hell am I supposed to do that? They're old. Do I photoshop my stupid selfie face on there?"

Uh oh.

We knew it the moment the words came out of my mouth. Yes. I'm supposed to photoshop my stupid selfie face on there. Do I know how to photoshop? Nope. Is it free? I don't think so. Damn it.

* * *

I have a FaceTime coffee with Michelle on Saturday. We were in the same executive master's degree cohort, so we know each other very well. We also wound up stuck in the Mexico City airport, having missed our connecting flights to Rebecca's wedding, and had to find a hotel and spend the night together. It was a really nice evening, if I'm honest. I should post a video from dinner on Instagram. Look at me, growing up and sharing...

"Just decide what you want to talk about on my podcast," she says ending an explanation of the format she uses.

"Ok, let me think about it. When I met with the guy who runs the book program a couple months ago, he told me he saw my book going into a podcast. I thought he was crazy because the last thing I wanted to do here was write a book, let alone do a podcast."

"I understand, but keep in mind everyone is taking on different roles right now. If you want to be a podcaster, be a podcaster. No one is going to give you permission. You just do it."

Uh oh. She's right. I haven't been in touch yet to tell her what I want to talk about on her podcast, but I've certainly been thinking about giving myself permission to be whoever the fuck I want to be. I don't suffer from a lack of confidence. If I got this, I got this.

But… I do suffer from imposter syndrome. I have to look up the difference between a disease and a syndrome. A disease is a medical condition. A syndrome is a collection of symptoms.

Yes, that's correct. I have imposter syndrome, and the symptoms are wreaking havoc on my system! Twenty minutes ago, I had to postpone recording my pre-launch video campaign because I ate so much crap over the last few days that I look like a puffer fish. Self-sabotage is an effective, yet brutal, form of procrastination.

I don't have the time to let my own bullshit get in my way.

PART 6

WHAT'S NEXT?

CHAPTER 25

BUY IN

———

Leap and the net will appear.

—ZEN SAYING

I've ignored people outside and inside my inner circle for a few weeks. No offense, but the only ones allowed in are my coach, editor, family, and those likely to pay me money. Everyone else has heard crickets.

A handful of people know this is classic Julie behavior. I'm back in racehorse gear with satin blinders on. And let me tell you, these have been an ugly couple of weeks. I made a tremendous pivot and somehow convinced really smart people that my idea has merit, but not without sleepless nights and an angry stomach. Pink is my favorite TUMS flavor now, which I give a five-star rating and highly recommend.

A friend left me two voice messages (ignored), a missed FaceTime call, and a missed regular call all within an hour of each other. Either something was going down and he needed a friend, or he was tired of my racehorse routine. Thankfully, nothing bad was happening in his life—just in mine.

DEFIANT is on the edge. I'm changing course by adding a ton of work and going in a direction I know barely anything about, and I'm scared. I know I can execute like a mother-fucker on this shift. No doubt. I'll put my head down and plow through until it starts to happen. (The line separating work horse and racehorse is not well marked.)

My fear is in the opportunity cost. It's just about the only term from Business Management 101 freshman year I remember. It's this equation: if you do x, you do not have the ability to do y. I love to think I'm invincible and can do x, y, and z. The truth, though, is that the first draft of this book is due to the publisher four weeks from tomorrow. My pivot has a cliffhanger deadline merely three days before.

If I do the book (x) and the marketing funnel pivot (y), I do not have the ability to do z. No, I don't know what z is. Z is just the thing I won't have the time to do, and that scares me. I have to defer everything that isn't X or Y until late June—all other potential revenue, everything.

That's risky.

Not to be dramatic, but I have four months of runway left before I have to dip into my savings. Don't get excited about that account, folks, it's not going to keep this racehorse in fine style. Rationally, I know I'm making this pivot, and investing my energy and abilities in it for four weeks is a gamble.

So... I've been focused. I haven't done the productivity hacks I know could help, like making time blocks, because I've been busy standing on the edge. I am a little frozen, sure, but standing—just getting comfortable and feeling the wind. I am a horse on the edge of a cliff, not sure if she should back away and hunker down or go for the jump. What a weird picture!

This is not my first cliff, but I kind of thought I was done with this feeling. I had it back in December when DEFIANT opened her first bank account. I was in racehorse gear, and when I finally stopped moving long enough to prove to a bank that it was real, the emotions I was outrunning caught up to me. It was intense and a near fight with Andrew. He thought I should be excited, and I thought I should be institutionalized.

I am getting a little more comfortable, though. I've camped out for the last ten days on the edge—not a lot of changes. I can see a little clearer and a little further. It's not much, but the view is spec-fucking-tacular. Sometimes self-doubt rolls in, and I duck under Hulu. It's safer there, but it won't help me reach the other side.

My headspace is my priority, and I didn't want to talk to a close friend, one capable of calling me out. What if he thinks my pivot is nuts? I'd tossed it to a few people already, but he has seen me stumble and climb back up. It's a lot: a podcast, webinars, a mastermind, and courses. What if he thinks it's too much?

I don't want to talk about my stress because I'll just get overwhelmed and frustrated.

I call back on FaceTime and let him see my crazy—frizzy weird hair pulled back in a claw clip, glasses, tired face, and a tired voice to match. It is lovely. I am chastised for retreating and called out for going silent. It's all true. The thing that gave him the empathy to cut me a little slack was how pathetic I look. We agree to meet up in the morning to get coffee, and I go back to watching Hulu and searching Google for a reason to not pivot.

Why? Because it's nuts! Leaving my unfulfilling job for the entrepreneur life was a huge risk. Now I want to take another one? What the hell is wrong with me?

* * *

Shit.

Apparently, my pivot is not nutso-futso. It's still in the self-serve nut aisle at Whole Foods HQ in Austin, though. I judge all other Whole Foods by the variety and selection I see at HQ. It's so good I've had to exile myself. Just talking about it makes me want to go... but nothing good will come of it. Many delicious things, but no good. Adulting sucks.

I order an Americano this morning, and it is pretty good, not fresh peanut butter good, but good. The other good thing is the lack of negative feedback on my pivot. I explain the concept and the components of the funnel. I answer all his questions. Then the conversation moves to why I'd gone radio silent.

I roll my eyes.

I knew this was coming. He was smart enough to give me space over the last week or so, but he didn't know why I needed it. If he'd pressed me for an answer earlier this week, I wouldn't have had one.

It's not a unique reason. I just ran out of steam and couldn't regenerate at the speed I needed to. When AUSA cancelled our contract instead of rolling it into the next event, that closed a door. I'd mourned the loss of the event in June, but I hadn't processed the loss of the money. I was fucked.

All by myself, without my mobster buddha Tony's help, I'd done the emotional duct tape thing. I'd even managed to shove it into the trunk of my mental nineties Buick, but that just means I am taking it with me wherever I go. Until I had enough space between the phone call from AUSA and where I am now heading, I couldn't look at it. Finally, I am honest with them and explain that I didn't know how to handle it, logistically not emotionally, and we reach an agreement. I mail them a check.

It wasn't until I wrote that check—DEFIANT's first one, #5001—and dropped it in the mail did I bolt that door from my side. I am done. It's time to pivot.

* * *

Happy Memorial Day, dear laptop!

I just sent my first, admittedly pathetic, proposal for the funnel. I named the project "Hurry Up and Wait" because it's funny and a thing in the government/military. Folks are often called on to get something done ASAP, and then they wait. That emergency response never seems to find its way to the intended outcome. Unless, of course, it's an actual emergency, or war.

A week ago, I pitched a skeleton of it to Charlie, a contractor at AAL. He works for Cyclone, a government contract company, as a something or other. Who knows?

A couple weeks ago, Charlie shared an upcoming SBIR webinar Cyclone had planned on LinkedIn. Well, shucks, I could hardly resist! I attend, by way of my yoga mat, and think they did a great job of passing the mic and looking alive while discussing the driest topic on Zoom that day.

"Great job, team!" I send a group message to the three of them on LinkedIn.

Charlie writes back and asks if I would give them feedback. Oh, you want me to pay attention this time? Sure...

He sends me their first webinar from a couple weeks ago, and I watched it on double time, my favorite speed for SBIR content. Again, they do a great job. So, I reach out to schedule a conversation.

Today, we talk. I tell him about my pivot and the components of the funnel, and he loves it. We'll see if he's going to support it, and if so how, but for now I just need the validation. I think he would be the perfect cohost for the podcast because he is a good ying to my yang.

Remember a few months ago when I tried to tell Brett selling his tech to the military also involved making it fit in their specifications? I'd suggested he speak to an SBIR consultant about pursuing R&D dollars. Maybe we can start the podcast by having that conversation. No, not with Brett. That topic has value, especially for other potential defense entrepreneurs.

I think. We'll see.

CHAPTER 26

IMPOSTER SYNDROME

———

I know you're tired, but come, this is the way.

—RUMI

I recorded the promo video for the book pre-sale last weekend, and while the publisher does their editing magic, I get to overthink my performance.

First, the eyelashes were not home grown. I hope that doesn't ruin any preconceived notions about my ability to create gusts of wind when I blink. I arranged for my friend Jessica, who lives in my building, to help me get set up (a.k.a. use her condo). Why? To give me space from reality. I know it's stupid, but I want to keep my actual location private to all but those willing to dig just a little deeper.

That's not the only reason. Jessica was a television producer in New York City. If anyone knows how to light someone, it's her. She added lashes to my mascara, bronzer to my blush, and gloss to my lipstick.

"This is kind of intense. I mean, thank you, but this is a lot," I said.

She responded with, "You know, I have done this for really famous people."

I laughed. It was exactly the kind of comment I needed to crack the tension I walked in with. Yikes. I really wanted the video to strike the right tone—something about the importance of military modernization, something about controversy, and a lot about how it's not a "gotcha" book. Although, all of that is just me trying to cover up my imposter syndrome. Why else would I say it's not a gotcha book?

I would prefer if I'd managed to say, "it is a story of entrepreneurship," without my voice raising every time I say that word like a question. "Entrepreneurship?" It sounds like I'm questioning it, but I'm not. I just haven't accepted the label. It's like one of those stickers you get in the mail and leave it sitting on the kitchen counter for months. ASPCA, anyone? Well, I haven't peeled it off and put it on me yet.

Does that make sense? I'm six months into being an entrepreneur, according to the definition, but I'm also two months into a global pandemic and one month into pivoting my company. So, I don't know where to put the label. I don't know if it goes on me or the company.

Here's a little secret: I don't want to be an entrepreneur. They try and fail. Then they try again. Or they get funding. And then they have investors who want to apply influence because, you know, they paid for that privilege. I don't want that. I want to avoid that entire cycle, and if that means I don't identify as an entrepreneur then SO WHAT?

I didn't want to be a "founder" either, until I realized all the shit I was dealing with was because I'm a founder. Being a founder is hard. Stupid hard. You have to somehow know enough about everything to know when you're doing things correctly and what to do if you suspect you aren't. It's trial by the best of intentions. You try, but you don't have a flipping clue. Like that time I was close to becoming an international arms dealer. Remember way back in February? Oh, the good old days...

* * *

Damn you, Kyle! He told me I should hire two interns, and I thought he was insane. Why would I subject anyone to this? Especially young minds? They don't deserve it.

Then, Kyle got an intern, and he gushed on a call about the experience. Of course he would, Kyle's the nicest human being ever. So, I thought about it again and decided to reach out to Larry, my Georgetown University contact.

Larry was encouraging and lovely about it. He seemed to think Kyle's attempt to make a CEO out of me was a good investment. He also didn't get the impression I should be kept away from impressionable minds.

I disagree, but maybe I'm a cautionary tale? Hard to know.

After googling around for other people's podcast production internship postings, I stole 99 percent of one and changed some words. I would give them credit, but I closed that browser tab already. It's lost forever. Then, I went through the hoops of signing up as an employer (what?) on Handshake.

* * *

Full speed ahead on hiring an intern to be DEFIANT's podcast producer.

I do a quick scan of the first applicant and am filled with adoration. They (I'm using gender neutral pronouns because you don't need to know anything about this person) are unique and clearly driven. Based on the resume, they're interested in the national security side of things.

Here's what they applied for:

Build your portfolio!

DEFIANT is currently seeking podcast production interns interested in launching a new podcast. This opportunity requires self-motivation, a desire to gain experience in multiple disciplines, and a passion for national security/defense.

This is an ideal portfolio building opportunity for candidates who are not afraid to make mistakes (seriously), listen to a variety of current podcasts, and are seeking a career in content creation, media, entrepreneurship, etc. You—yes, you—will work directly with the founder and CEO, virtually, to schedule interviews, design questions and topics of discussion, research best practices, attract advertisers and sponsors, produce the podcast, monitor and analyze data, and make presentations.

Depending on your varying interests and skills, you will contribute to the planning & development of the podcasts, interviewing, editing, mixing, and publishing.

It was a pain in the booty to get approval from other schools to post jobs. Georgetown was on board, because Hoyas rule, but everyone else gave me canned messages about how they don't post babysitting jobs. Yep, my business address is also my home address. It's also my baby, but not in the babysitting sense.

Although, a babysitter for my business would be nice. What's the corporate term? COO?

CHAPTER 27

PODCAST

———

I just need to figure out how things work.

—IVAN SUTHERLAND

I'm noticing good and bad things hit me at the same time. I'm almost at the point where if something happens, good or bad, I start looking for the counterbalance. There is a ying to every yang.

For example, on the happy ying side, I'm getting applications for podcast producer interns, and they're overwhelmingly awesome. I'm starting to feel less reluctant to bringing in a student because I see the value in giving them the experience. Ahem, I mean sharing the experience.

Larry told me the closer students can get to the founder, the better for them. It makes some sense, but I'm not convinced I should be allowed to inflict DEFIANT on impressionable minds.

It's the space between starting something new and being an imposter. I want to stay on the side where I embrace new projects and identities, obviously.

On my return to WeWork last Monday I passed a guy on a bench. He made a comment about liking my dress, and I thanked him. On Tuesday I saw the same man on the same bench. I said hello, and he invited me to sit across from him. I did. We chatted. He dropped a few nuggets about what he does and who he is. He had me look him up on Google. Who does that?

"All I see is you with a bunch of blondes."

He laughed.

"Same ones?" I asked.

"No."

He dangled an opportunity for me to work with him on a fundraising campaign for health care in minority communities. George Floyd was murdered a week and a half before we met, and the conversation about health disparity had reached mainstream news. Of course, I was interested in a chance to add value to this cause by amplifying it.

That night I looked deeper at his organization. My conclusion was that it is clickbait, hence the blondes, with no substance. He used name recognition of a medical journal as leverage. How do I explain this…? In the strategic communications world, I'd give him a C+. He knew enough about the game to know how to get attention, but he never had the goods to back it up.

The photos of the blondes were three years old. The journal he supposedly edited was his blog, not the real medical journal. His organization was not really a nonprofit. It didn't check out.

He is a real imposter. I am not. Time to tell imposter syndrome to take a hike off the cliff.

* * *

Now for the yang side. I foolishly open LinkedIn and discover that AFWERX has launched a podcast. Cue the sucker punch sound. That was my idea! This is my pivot! They can't have my pivot! I mean… they didn't steal it; they're just doing what I'm doing and jumping on a great opportunity.

This afternoon, Downtown Randy Clark and I took our caffeine, courtesy of WeWork, to one of the many faux living rooms. We assumed our regular positions: Randy with one ankle crossed over the other knee displaying his tight sneaker game, and me curled up in a ball on my side with my Rothy's hanging off. My mother would be proud. Randy's body language was open, and I was protective.

As an entrepreneur, it's hard to share your ideas. So much depends on their success (so much… so, so much), and sometimes other people don't realize how much. Constructive feedback is a gift. Idea squashing is not.

"Okay. Here's what I'm thinking…" I trail off. Whatever I'm thinking is stuck. Randy just sits there. He's seen this before.

"Okay. Let me try again. Um… so…" I exhale.

I inhale.

"Okay. I realize I'm not saying anything. But… I think I just feel uncertain about things."

I take another inhale.

"You know how when generals want to try something new, they first pitch it to think tanks in the UK?"

Randy just looks at me.

"Okay. Think about it. Our generals 'accept' a speaking engagement in London, and then they come back with some new great idea, right?"

"That's true. Lieutenant General Wesley spends a lot of time in the UK."

I wait. He's starting to see where I'm going.

"They go overseas to get the UK, Canada, New Zealand, and Australia," I catch myself explaining the five eyes (FVEYs) intelligence sharing alliance to an insider. "I'm sorry, Randy, of course you know FVEYs... where is my head today? They go pitch it to FVEYs and other strategic allies to get buy in before pitching it here. It's not the only reason they're there or that they have those conversations, but our military modernization generals are talking to our allies. It adds credibility to the idea or next step. Why don't I do that? Take the podcast overseas. Then, I can bypass all the bureaucracy here and talk to companies and learn how other countries are doing it."

"Um, can you even travel right now? What about the ecosystem here? Isn't Capital Factory doing a virtual event in lieu of FUTURES coming up?" he asks.

"There's an event every day. It's exhausting to keep up. You mean Fed Supernova? I don't know. I haven't heard back from them about the stipend and frankly, I don't want to do it. I'm tired of being asked to participate because I'm fun and pretty."

Randy is confused. "You're not fun and pretty! I mean... you're not *just* fun and pretty. Why would you say that?"

Laughing, I say, "I didn't tell you?"

"Tell me what?" He looks horrified. Remember when I told you he's the embodiment of a golden retriever? He would never think of a woman as just fun and pretty, nor would he select her to host a virtual conference based on those qualities.

Except, that's exactly what happened. "I asked why they were reaching out to me and the answer was, 'because you're fun and pretty,'" I say in my best dude voice.

"Julie... wow..."

I broke Randy. Shoot. I want to talk about changing the trajectory of the podcast to outside the United States so I wouldn't be just another voice on military modernization in this country. My producer intern starts June 25—three days after my manuscript goes to the publisher—and I want to have some idea of what I'm doing.

In addition to AFWERX, all the think tanks have joined the podcast bandwagon. I'm not trying to compete with think tanks. Those conversations are high-level, and you need an advanced degree in security studies or Chinese/Russian relations to keep up. I don't know exactly what my value proposition is, though, and I like the idea of having a wider perspective than just ours (or Austin's).

Eventually, Randy and I find our way back to the topic of doing an international podcast.

Randy, going straight for the tactical question, asks, "How would you get generals from other countries to talk to you?"

"That's the beauty of it. I won't. I want the policy makers, lobbyists, tech companies, big defense companies, and AUSA-equivalents to talk to me. I don't have to stay in Austin, or even in the United States, to fight my way through our bureaucratic bullshit. I can vacation in someone else's bullshit!"

There is plenty of space for more than one podcast, and even more space for me because I want to make this specifically for defense entrepreneurs. Also, I don't have the censors AFWERX and think tanks do. I can call a spade a spade. They could maybe say it is "spade-like" or "performs a similar function of a spade," but not me.

You know, it's just like how it's basically a requirement to buy an MOU in order to get into the R&D funding pipeline of the SBIR process. Isn't that a pretty little spade? Look what we can dig up with that one!

Let's go find spades, in spades. Let's go see how modernization is done elsewhere and talk to the companies doing it. At a minimum, can I just bust out of this stupid corrupt shed and go find an airport lounge to hang out in?

CHAPTER 28

UNFUCK IT, PLEASE

In the middle of difficulty lies opportunity.

—ALBERT EINSTEIN

I did not get the nod from the governor's office to get the $125K to conduct SBIR outreach in Texas.

Thank goodness!

I had a call with them last week on Friday. I was transparent that I don't have experience managing a grant, and I don't want to. I want to do the thing and help with the stuff, but I don't give a flying flute about oversight. Providing performance metrics and accounting for the sake of bureaucrats checking boxes is not consistent with my brand. [wink]

No, thank you.

They called yesterday to tell me, informally, they were not moving forward with my proposal. Obviously. We were on the same page when we hung up from that call on Friday. I'm a value-add on someone else's proposal. I'm not stand-alone.

Cool. I just needed to know if they could see what I could see.

I asked. "Do you think it will work? The podcast and the funnel?"

"Yes, we do."

My jaw dropped a little. That was all I needed to know.

* * *

A podcast is cool, but... what's next?

At this point, you've been with me through starting DEFI-ANT, the first few months of my lounge-hopping lifestyle, the crash bang boom of COVID-19, and what it took to figure out how to move forward.

You've also had a front row seat to both sides of the SBIR equation. You know how it is incentivized and that companies pay for access to signatories with tremendous influence on how federal R&D dollars are spent. The weight of MOUs in the equation nullifies the layers attempting to enforce open competition in government contracts.

A podcast isn't going to fix that. The entire funnel I've come up with is lovely, but it's not enough. As long as the MOUs have weight, the system is rigged. Entrepreneurs have the magic, and Uncle Sam has the money; however, payola decides which tools the next generation of warfighters will have (not the technical feasibility).

It's entirely possible you won't care about this. Why should you? There are many problems we could tackle together. We could fight on climate change, human trafficking, and opioid addiction. I'm down for that, but I need to figure out a way through this problem first.

The obvious answer is to discontinue allowing for MOUs on Phase 1 proposals, that way the true purpose of Phase 1— to determine if the project is possible—would be restored to its former glory. Providing our warfighters with cool shit that works is… the whole idea.

Unfortunately, I don't have that kind of power.

Don't worry. I think I've met a few people in the first six months of DEFIANT who can intercept payola and take the power those MOUs have away. One of those people popped into my head today as I was trying to think of a way out of this for all of us (cue the angels).

At noon today I have a meeting with Noah, the man who will be responsible for implementing my evil little plan. He has created a few secure websites for the military and several artificial intelligence algorithms already. In addition, he understands my frustration with the MOUs and the SBIR market.

Since this book won't be published for a few months, I suppose I can tell you about the idea I've hatched and how I see partnering with Noah. Ready?

To make the MOU black market irrelevant, I'm going to ask Noah today to create a database that connects defense entrepreneurs with the people they need to talk to. It's not rocket science, but there will be resistance. There are many reasons for that, but for now let's just look at a potential solution and be hopeful.

I bet Noah can help me democratize access to the network and give entrepreneurs the power to make the connections without paying for them. If I learned anything in the first quarter of 2020, it's that defense entrepreneurs have more solutions than they can transfer into warfighter hands. If I learned anything in the second quarter of 2020, it's that there is a flaw in the system. I hope the rest of 2020 teaches me that we can fix it.

Dear Warfighter,

Hey, how's war?

I was just thinking about you and wanted to check in. Things are good here.

A lot of cool stuff could be headed your way soon. Lives will be saved... maybe even yours?

One quick thing, while you've been gone, we kind of fucked things up, so that cool stuff is stuck.

If you get a minute, can you help us unfuck it, please?

Love,

Julie

ACKNOWLEDGEMENTS

To the brave souls who bought this book sight unseen: thank you. Your support made it possible.

Alan G. Badgley
Amber Allen
Amy Kluber
Angela Betancourt
Anna N. McClure
Brandon Stevens
Chad Vanderslice
Chris Angarita
Clark Dutterer
Cris Medina
Daniel Hargrove
David Johnson
Deborah Finch
Denise Amato
Eric Koester
Frank Roan
Greg Johnston
Heather Price

Jefery Spangler
Jennifer Gilbert
Jessie Wilson
Jim and Nancy Finkbeiner
John Martinez
John and Sarah Gamino
Jonathan Josephson
Jonathan Lirette
Jordan LaCrosse
Joshua Rentrope
Julia McAdams
Karen Bishop
Karen Rickey
Karla Heren
Kate Arredondo
Kelsey Buchanan
Kevin Landtroop
Launtz Rodgers

Lesley Wilhelm
Linda Deppe
Lori Wulf
Luke Shabro
Mack McCarter
Mark Johnson
Matthew Creedican
Melissa Mahoney
Melissa Warnke
Meredith Morse
Michael Kurland
Michele Kolbas
Nicholas D'Souza
Nicole Deterding
Patrick Enright
Pramod Raheja
Raymond Kaminski

Robert Douthit
Robert Katz
Robyn Finkbeiner
Russ and Bev Stubbles
Ryan P. Conner
Sally Kenyon Grant
Scott Nelson
Shane Smith
Sharon Krohn
Shayna Cherry
Somer Hackley
Susan Sloan
Thomas Bradley
Thomas Gromus
Tracey Ference
Tricia Perez
Zac Staples

APPENDIX

CHAPTER 5

Linder, Jason N. PsyD. "What the Heck is EMDR Therapy? Can It Really Help Me?" Psychology Today, July 19, 2020. https://www.psychologytoday.com/us/blog/relationship-and-trauma-insights/202007/what-the-heck-is-emdr-therapy-can-it-really-help-me

CHAPTER 9

Internal Revenue Service. (2017). Form 990: Return of Organization Exempt from Income Tax: Association of the United States Army Inc. Retrieved from the ProPublica database. https://projects.propublica.org/nonprofits/organizations/530193361/201843199349313774/full

Internal Revenue Service. (2016). Form 990: Return of Organization Exempt from Income Tax: Association of the United States Army Inc. Retrieved from the ProPublica database.

https://projects.propublica.org/nonprofits/organiza-tions/530193361/201703199349313995/full

CHAPTER 10

Burden, Colonel Patrick W. "Acquisition Reform—What's Really Broken in Defense Acquisition." (Senior Service College Fellowship Civilian Research Project, U.S. Army War College, 2010). 1-42.

"Geopolitics and Government Affairs." Berlin Global Advisors. Accessed September 1, 2020.

"Lieutenant General (Ret'd) Ben Hodges." Royal United Services Institute (RUSI). Accessed August 31, 2020.

"Overview of the Federal Procurement Process and Resources." EveryCRSReport. January 16, 2015.

Vandiver, John. "How US Army Europe's outgoing general got the Pentagon's attention." STARS AND STRIPES. October 17, 2017.

ACRONYM LIST

AAL – Army Applications Laboratory
AFC – Army Futures Command
AUSA – Association of the United States Army
ASAP – As Soon As Possible
ASPCA – American Society for the Prevention of Cruelty
to Animals

BAA – Broad Agency Announcement
BD – Business Development

CBD - Cannabidiol
CFO – Chief Financial Officer
CG – Commanding General
CI – Counterintelligence
CIO – Chief Information Officer
CISO – Chief Information Security Officer
COL – Colonel
COO – Chief Operations Officer
CSM – Command Sergeant Major
CSO – Chief Strategy Officer
CTO – Chief Technology Officer

DCA – Ronald Reagan National Airport
DIU – Defense Innovation Unit
DOD – Department of Defense
DUNS – Data Universal Numbering System

EMDR – Eye Movement Desensitization and Reprocessing
ERCA – Extended Range Canon Artillery

FAR – Federal Acquisition Register
FAST – Federal and State Technology
FBI – Federal Bureau of Investigation
FBO/FedBizOpps – Federal Business Opportunities
FVEY – Five Eyes

GPS – Global Positioning System
GRU – Glavnoye Razvedyvatel'noye Upravleniye
GSA – Government Services Administration

H2F – Holistic Health and Fitness
HIIT – High Intensity Interval Training
HQ - Headquarters
HST – Harry S. Truman (building)
HUMINT – Human Intelligence

IC – Intelligence Community
IG – Inspector General
iPEC – Institute for Professional Excellence in Coaching
ITARs – International Traffic in Arms Regulations

J2 - Joint Warfighting Capabilities Assessments for Intelligence, Surveillance, and Reconnaissance

MBDA – Minority Business Development Agency
MG – Major General
MOU – Memorandum of Understanding

NASA – National Aeronautics and Space Administration
NATO – North Atlantic Treaty Organization
NDA – Non-Disclosure Agreement
NDAA – National Defense Authorization Act
NGO – Non-Governmental Organization
NSIN – National Security Innovation Network

OPSEC – Operational Security
Org - Organization

PAO – Public Affairs Officer
PMP – Project Management Professional
PPP – Payment Protection Program
PR – Public Relations
PTAP – Procurement Technical Assistance Program
PTL – Personnel Tracking Locator

R&D – Research and Development
RCCTO – Army Rapid Capabilities and Critical Technologies Office

SAM – System for Award Management
SBA – Small Business Administration
SBIR – Small Business Innovation Research
SecArmy – Secretary of the Army
SFC – Sergeant First Class
STTR – Small Business Technology Transfer
SXSW – South by Southwest

TSA – Transportation Security Administration

UFO – Unidentified Flying Object
USG – United States Government
UT – University of Texas

5Ws – Who, What, Where, When, and Why